'The author herself . . . is resolutely anti-miserable, always cracking jokes. Her account of the attack is unblinking, matter of fact and occasionally sardonic. "It was when he started strangling me that I realized it wasn't a social call," she tells a police officer who interviews her afterwards. She has stern things to say about rape conviction rates, pathetically low in this country, and about police procedure and the judicial system . . . Describing her recovery, she manages to convey the loneliness of it without even so much as a hint of self-pity.'

Rachel Cooke, *Observer*

'The book is an eloquent appeal, to men and women, to change their thinking about rape and sexual assault.'

Alexandra Blair, *The Times*

'It brings to life something that many women fear: not just becoming the victim of a sex attack but the endless frustration of trying to ensure that the perpetrator is brought to justice. There is a crisis about sexual violence in this country, with most rapists fully aware of how unlikely they are to be convicted. *Words Can Describe* is vivid, frank and courageous, and I'm sure many women will be grateful to Abi Grant for telling the truth at, I imagine, some cost to herself.'

Joan Smith

'What was surprising and a bit unexpected was the way in which things that are often demonised in the press were shown as fundamental to her recovery. Rarely have I come across a depiction of someone living in a one-bed council flat on incapacity benefit shown in such a positive, life-affirming light . . . As an articulate, white, professional woman who was attacked in her own home by a total stranger, her case should have been more straightforward than most, but even in this "textbook" case she found herself attacked in court and her sexual history and that of her flatmate called into doubt. But despite the horrible thing that happened to her, she always manages to place it within a much wider context . . . I'm really glad I read this book.'

Socialist Review

'It reveals the truth about coping with the trauma of rape, and calls for urgent change to the legal system . . . A clear-eyed, coruscating description of the attack committed by Strachan and its dreadful, life-altering aftermath, it's more than a personal story of survival. Starting with a dedication to Stacey Westbury, a 23-year-old raped and murdered in her London home in 2007, and ending with a list of ten tips for dealing with traumatised people ("Don't pretend you understand by introducing a bad experience of your own. Getting raped isn't the same as when your mother died"), the book is Grant's attempt to fracture the silence that surrounds rape; to challenge the myths around sexual violence, that women ask for it, or deserve it. And most of all it's a call to action.'

Scotsman

Words Can Describe

Abi Grant is by profession a writer, for stage and TV, and contributes regularly to the *Daily Telegraph*. Her original piece on the rape case was a lead article for the *Observer* Magazine and as a result she received a vast mailbag.

Words Can Describe

ABI GRANT

PICADOR

First published 2009 by Picador

This edition first published 2010 by Picador
an imprint of Pan Macmillan, a division of Macmillan Publishers Limited
Pan Macmillan, 20 New Wharf Road, London N1 9RR
Basingstoke and Oxford
Associated companies throughout the world
www.panmacmillan.com

ISBN 978–0-330–51835–2

Visit **www.picador.com** to read more about all our books
and to buy them. You will also find features, author interviews and
news of any author events, and you can sign up for e-newsletters
so that you're always first to hear about our new releases.

Following a tragedy, you'll invariably see a distraught relative on the news outside the law courts or a hospital, choking back tears saying, 'Words cannot describe how I feel.'

At this point I always find myself yelping at the screen, 'Oh yes they can – that's exactly *what words can do.' What I think people mean is, there are no easy similes to describe how they feel. Having your child murdered or seeing a mate blown up by a roadside bomb isn't 'like' anything else. Neither is waking up to find a serial rapist in your bedroom.*

But I'm giving words a go.

Chapter One

Life being what it is, one dreams of revenge.

PAUL GAUGUIN

THE FIRST THING that struck me was what a little man he was. Not just short, but petty and nondescript. When he sat he slumped forward, which made him look even smaller. His institutional grey sweatshirt matched his hair and sallow complexion, and I agreed with myself that of the two of us, I had aged better. I was aware of voices gabbling as proceedings began, but kept my eyes on him, with the kind of open glare that in a pub or schoolyard would precipitate a fight. And I felt a strong urge to fight him. More specifically I felt a strong urge to punch him in the face bone-creakingly hard. It was the atavistic call of unfinished business. Eventually he looked up and caught my eye, more by accident than purpose. I dead-eyed him (you looking at me?) and his eyes flicked nervously down and away. Ha, I thought, not so tough now, are we? I childishly reckoned I could take him, and more adultly, that if I had a tyre iron, there'd be blood on the floor.

We'd met once before.

It was January 1993. I was twenty-eight years old and had written the book for a musical. After years in the TV sketch-show salt mines, this was my First Big Thing and I'd given it my all. Unfortunately, after a six-month sell-out run in Birmingham, the show arrived in the West End just in time for the last great IRA bombing campaign on the mainland. It wasn't just the bombs, it was the warnings coming in at two or three a week. The West End ground to a halt, and everything closed that Christmas, a dozen or more shows in all.

The last Friday, cast, crew, chorus and orchestra all met at a restaurant in the Strand, and although it didn't start out as the happiest of evenings, in my experience if you put enough gay men and enough alcohol together a party will happen.

The gathering broke up in dribs and drabs around half-past three, with people crying and saying their goodnights, knowing that after Saturday's final performances our extended family would scatter, clearing their dressing rooms, packing up their good-luck cards, promising to keep in touch, but never really doing so.

I left the restaurant with Phil, the show's 'swing' tap-dancer. A stocky young man from a mining village in the North (Billy Eliot before there ever was one), we'd bonded during rehearsals, when I was complaining about a writer's lot. 'You try telling your dad you want to be a chorus boy,' he said and I knew we'd get on. I shivered in the evening chill, and he draped his coat over me, darting across the road to hail a cab from the other side. He saw me into it and we sadly said goodbye. As the cab drove home I realized that after three years' grindingly hard work, it really was all over bar the shouting.

It was bumping 4.00 a.m. when I got home. As I paid the cab driver, a tall cheerful black boy – an obvious party straggler – strolled up. 'Got a spare ciggie?' he asked. Having just waved goodbye to my First Big Thing, I was in a grimly giving mood – why the hell not. So I pulled out my Silk Cut. 'Excellent,' he grinned, 'my brand!' I gave him two. He asked me for a light, tucked the other behind his ear, thanked me and loped contentedly off towards Canonbury.

I trumped downstairs to my flat, checked my messages (none), wandered into the kitchen to make a cup of tea and then, overcome by exhaustion, tore off my clothes, letting them fall to the floor, pulled on a T-shirt and slid into bed and a deep sleep.

My police statement takes it from there:

I was then awoken with a start. I realised that the duvet had been pulled off and there was a man on top of me. I was flat on my back and he was flat on me. His chest was on my chest, and his face was inches from mine. I was pinned down and my arms were by my side.

I didn't believe it and shut my eyes. Despite feeling his breath on my face, it took several desperate 'peekings' before I realized, *This is happening . . .*

The man was rocking backwards and forwards as if he was simulating sex, and was trying to force my legs open with his legs. I was for about 15 seconds paralysed with fear.

My eyes hadn't adjusted to the dull light seeping through my blinds. All I could make out was a shape, dark, shifting and violent. He jabbed his tongue in my mouth, and I could taste the cigarettes. He grabbed my left breast through my T-shirt and began violently twisting it. 'No,' I whispered and I think, 'please.' My voice didn't work. 'Shut up, you fucking bitch, or I'll kill you,' he said, his voice working fine. The swearing and threats continued as he began punching me in the face, his erection grinding into me, his excitement building.

Then he stopped punching me and, holding me down with his left hand still squeezing my breast, he tried to insert the fingers of his right hand into me, but I kept my legs shut. There was no way he could force them, so he leaned back, grabbed my pubic hair. 'You cunt.'

I was absolutely petrified, but I realised my arms were half free, so I realised it could be my chance to get away. His trousers were pulled down and he was trying to direct his penis into my vagina.

His tracksuit bottoms were around his knees (he wasn't wearing underwear), and lying on top of me, he kept trying to force his dick in. I kept my legs tightly shut, and felt his erection against my thighs, jabbing against my pubis bone. Then he let go of my breast, shifted his weight to his left and used his right hand to 'guide' himself in.

I realised my left arm was half free, so I tried to grab his penis.

I missed, brushing it enough to feel its sponginess, but unable to grab it. Incensed, he reared up. He forced me back onto the bed, one hand squeezed around my throat, the other punching my face, spitting out threats with each blow.

He hit me at least ten times. He just kept punching me.

It wasn't until this moment that I consciously registered, 'He's strangling me with one hand, and hitting me with the other – he isn't armed.' I started wriggling wildly, trying to breathe and managing to deflect at least half the blows from my face to the side of my head.

The struggle became quite violent.

Pushing his chest with my right hand, I punched his face wildly with my left. He pressed harder against my throat and I thought I was going to die. No, not die, be killed. Thinking you're about to be murdered is beyond frightening. A rollercoaster or a near-miss in a car might set the pulses racing, but it isn't even on the same scale as being conscious that you soon may cease to exist.

What happened next was downright hallucinatory. Time expanded sideways. Facts, figures, people, places appeared not in a sequence but as one great moment of 'knowing'. I have a vivid memory of a photograph taken when I was a child. I can still see the garden, the boy playing a guitar, dappled sunlight falling on a fat man on a sun-lounger, and an apple tree in the background. It's as real a memory as anything that happened that night.

I've come to believe your life flashing in front of your eyes is the brain scrolling through everything that's ever happened to you, looking for a way out. Like you've Googled the word 'help'.

I 'woke' with one simple thought – let him get on with it and live (advice that was bandied around at that time). So I stopped struggling and lay completely still. It seemed to work. He stopped hitting me and let go of my throat. As I struggled for breath, he lifted up my shirt, and took his time to feel me, grabbing my right breast and twisting, and not swearing but moaning, 'Oh, yeah.' As he started to part my legs I had another simple thought. 'I'm going to be raped.' And then just as simply, 'I don't want to be raped.' So when he turned his attention back to my face, stroking my hair and putting his tongue in my mouth . . .

I bit it as hard as I could. The man screamed out and moved off me slightly . . .

I saw an opening and lunged for his dick. This time I made it, and felt a surge of hope as I squeezed, yanked and dug my nails in and he went berserk. I can't remember being hit – all I was thinking was, 'I'm not letting go.' At some point he tired of punching me or maybe the pain got too great. Anyway I saw another opening and using his dick for leverage, I hauled myself up into a sitting position.

And then I managed to head butt him.

As hard as I could.

He went 'Arrgh' and leapt backwards, he had loosed (sic) his erection and jumped back and ran out of the room.

It wasn't a tidy head-butt – I just threw my head at his, but on contact I recoiled back onto the bed, partly concussed, and when I sat up, I was alone.

Still wearing only a T-shirt, I ran out of the bedroom, through the living room to the front door, desperate to escape. I grabbed the door, but it was locked, which didn't make sense. If someone's in your flat they must've come in through the front door, right?

I remembered I'd dropped my keys next to the kettle in the kitchen when I'd made the tea. A new sickening fear grabbed me – I was trapped, and still had no idea where he was. I darted back to the living room and

grabbed an old swordstick I kept tucked behind the TV.
It was a rickety old thing from the 1920s, picked up as a
curio, but holding the two-foot steel blade, I immediately
felt stronger. I knew if he came back in I would try and
kill him. Still operating on simple thoughts, I stood square
to the kitchen door. 'If he comes in, go for the torso.'
One . . . two . . . Nothing.

All I could hear was my own blood pumping and
ragged breaths. I grabbed the phone and dialled 999, but
there was no line. The wire had been cut. I looked down
and there, laid out neatly on the floor, in descending
order of size, were the knives from the knife block in the
kitchen.

Stock-still, I held my breath to listen properly, then
hearing nothing ran into the kitchen for the keys. The
window above the sink was open, the bits and pieces from
the windowsill scattered. He'd left the same way he'd
come in. I shut the window and grabbed my keys. I was
shaking as I hauled on clothes then ran upstairs to my land-
lady, Peri. I pounded so hard on her door that I left marks
in the wood.

*I was in a terrible state. I was hysterical and sobbing
uncontrollably, I was physically shaking.*

She let me in, and phoned the police. It was all over in
under fifteen minutes.

*

Fifteen minutes later at about 6.00 a.m. the police car arrived and the machine took over. A male PC wiped blood off my face with a tissue and asked me to 'take him through what'd happened', while the other took my keys and went downstairs to check the premises.

The PC who stayed with me became very excited when I mentioned the black lad and the cigarettes. 'Describe him,' he said. 'But the man who attacked me was white,' I said. 'Yeah, but describe him anyway.'

Peri gave me a drink and handfuls of arnica and Ibuprofen, as the policeman dropped the tissues in the kitchen bin and radioed his colleague. (Peri quickly retrieved the tissues, thinking they might contain evidence.) Another police car arrived and I was driven to the station. On the way a third policeman asked me what had happened.

Dawn was breaking as we pulled into the police-station car park, and, entering through the back, we weaved our way through corridors to a neon-lit doctor's office. The policemen waited outside and I joined a weary-looking male doctor, seemingly unaffected or even interested in my distressed condition. 'We don't have any orange sticks,' he explained and used a blunt-edged piece of plastic to scrape under my nails. I felt at the time it wasn't working but didn't say, 'Why don't you do it properly?' because complaining was beyond my reach. The docility of being a victim is subtle and conditional, you fall into it without really knowing why.

After a tentative knock on the door two policewomen

entered, concern etched on their faces, and for the first time since it had all began, someone in uniform asked me how I *was*. 'OK,' I said, 'OK,' which comparatively was true. Their presence in the room meant the examination could proceed.

The doctor asked me to 'pop' my trousers down and lie on the bed, and for the second time in a hour, my body was exposed to a complete stranger. He checked for bruises on my thighs, quickly combed my pubic hair, then, after taking a blood sample for an AIDS test, quickly examined my face. 'Oh,' he said matter-of-factly, 'your nose is broken.' Without asking permission, he pinched the bridge between his first finger and thumb and clicked it back into place.

Peri arrived in another police car, bringing with her some fresh clothes, and once the examination was over, I was led to the only changing room they had in the station – the women's toilet.

The policewomen asked me to put everything I was wearing into large brown-paper evidence bags and then left me to it, guarding the door. I was alone. Standing half-dressed in the cubicle I staggered as I tried to change. I was present, but I wasn't – shock was settling in, vagueness descending and I began a bizarre monosyllabic commentary: 'That's the door – have to open the door … right … put the bag on the floor … right.' This disorientating dreamlike state was my first taste of what I would later come to know as 'dissociation'.

Digging through the bag Peri had brought, I pulled out

some grey jogging bottoms, a T-shirt and a cotton polo-neck jumper. But no pants or bra.

'Can I keep the pants. Peri didn't bring me any pants,' I called through the door, adding hopefully, 'I didn't put them on till after.'

Profuse apologies came from the other side. No, they needed the pants – forensic evidence might have got from him onto me, and from me onto the pants. Damn.

I pulled on the jogging bottoms, conscious that under loose baggy clothing I was naked. And without a bra my breasts were free to swing and move, which wouldn't bother me at home on my own, but I wouldn't even answer the door like that, let alone be in the company of strangers.

'Are you OK?'

'Yeah, thanks.'

I took a deep breath and peered in the mirror under the neon light. Could be worse. Nose was a funny shape – flatter across the bridge. The right eye was puffing up – massive bruise on my chin. I washed the blood off my cheek. Frankly, I thought it would be worse. Pushing my hair back with my Alice band, I winced. Ah! My strug-gling had forced his blows onto the right side of my skull, where a Pyrenean line of bruises was forming under my hairline. I washed my face, then blew my nose, surprised by the blobs of partly coagulated blood that flew out, and my nose started bleeding again.

'You need some help?'

'No, I'm ready.'

Toilet paper held to my nose, I braced myself for the

next round. I exited the toilet, handed them the evidence bags and was pleased to be given a brown-plastic vending cup of sweet tea in return. They said someone, I don't know, a superintendent or such, wanted to see me. I can't remember what rank he was, but I got the impression I was meant to understand this showed they were taking this seriously.

I was led into large room where six or seven police officers in full uniform were waiting. They settled down and to my unease, I realized I was expected to sit at the front.

Peri was brought in looking distressed and we exchanged glances, and then a middle-aged man in a crumpled suit and unkempt hair (suggesting only an hour ago he'd been as fast asleep as me) came in and offered me his sympathies. Superintendent or whatever he was pulled up a chair next to me. 'Oh God,' I thought, 'he's going to ask me to take him through what happened. And I've got no pants on.' And so, in a strange parody of a chat show, he asked me to take him through what had happened, every now and again interjecting questions.

I told them the evening had started at a restaurant, where I'd been celebrating/commiserating the end of the musical with cast and crew.

Had I been drinking?

Surprised to be asked, I said, 'Yes, I must have drunk a bottle and a half over the course of the evening' (which is actually in my statement).

Did I notice anyone watching me, when I left the restaurant, anyone lurking?

'No, no,' I said, 'only the cast, the streets were empty.' I continued, describing my waiting with Phil to get the cab, the ride home and the black boy asking me for cigarettes.

The room sat to attention. This black man. Could I describe him?

I said he was about twenty to twenty-five years, but the man who attacked me was white.

'Yes, but describe him anyway.'

I said, he was upbeat, he was grinning, partly at his own cheek, but also his stroke of luck at finding someone to cadge a fag off at that time of the morning. I said he reminded me of half the boys I went to school with. Nothing dodgy about him at all. In fact I liked him, that's why I gave him two.

'Yes, but what did he look like?'

Oh, *that* kind of description. I said he was five foot nine inches tall, with short Afro hair, wearing a brown jacket – not bomber, more like a tux – and casual clothes.

There was a lot of scribbling in the room, so I said again, 'The man who attacked me was *white*.'

'Yes, but this man might be a witness,' said the suit.

Did the man who attacked me have an accent? Tattoos? Any physical marks or distinguishing features?

I told them he was in his twenties, and he was muscular, but wiry, about the same height and build as an ex-boyfriend – he wasn't a six-footer, and he wasn't heavy.

'What about his hair?'

That was either short or tied back – if it had been long I would've grabbed it.

'Could you taste anything?'

The wince-making questions. There's a reason why prostitutes don't kiss, it's too intimate. I closed my eyes. I said I could taste tobacco and what I thought was alcohol. He had a rough face, quite angular with some stubble, thin lips and a small thin tongue.

'What did he smell like?'

Skanky – sweaty, like he needed a bath.

'What was he wearing?'

As I was bouncing back onto the mattress, he was pulling up his tracksuit bottoms. They were black, blue maybe – all I saw was white cock and thighs against dark material – no underwear (meaning he came prepared for rape, this was no burglary 'gone wrong' as the police put it). And cold metal on my stomach, probably a zip off a tracksuit top, pressing into me.

There were moments of frantic scribbling when I said something relevant, but otherwise the atmosphere was as subdued as the neon light was harsh. As I went on to describe, not just the violence, but the order of the violence, I had a squawking sense that I was disappearing, and another me was taking my place. I wanted it to be over.

When I reached the part where I head-butted him, I tried to explain that I wasn't brave, I was desperate, but several officers muttered, 'Good one,' and the suit congratulated me.

'It was when he started strangling me,' I added, 'that I realized it wasn't a social call.'

Only one policeman laughed, or rather sniggered at the back. I'm not sure why I said it – I think I needed to know I was still alive, that the me beneath the bruises and blood was still there. At least it deflected talk of 'bravery'. I'd rather be thought peculiar than brave.

Twenty minutes later, we were finished and the meeting broke up, the police dispersed and it was time to be driven home – they'd take my statement later. I didn't want to go home. I liked being in a police station, I felt unequivocally safe. Despite having been attacked by a man, I liked the manliness of the police, uniformed up, bristling with badges and radios. They were on *my* side. Coupled with Peri's hawkish motherly protection, I would've happily sat quietly in a corner for a couple of hours. But instead we were driven 'home' to Peri's during the morning rush hour, and I gazed bewilderedly at people waiting at bus stops, reading papers, life carrying on. Hadn't the world just changed? Of course it hadn't. Mine had, that was all.

Inside the car, the policemen chatted amiably about what they could get him for. 'Now let's see,' said one, 'there's B&E . . .' (breaking and entering). 'GBH?' he said, looking to the second officer hopefully.

'Maybe,' said the other, 'ABH, definitely.'

'Right, so B&E, GB/ABH, sexual assault . . .'

Nothing compartmentalizes suffering like the law.

'Theft?'

'Yeah, he'll have nicked something . . .'

The chitchat continued, along with reassurances that they'd catch him and that when they did, he'd be sorry. ('We call it "resisting arrest".') I knew they were just trying to make me feel better, but, dizzy and tired, my attention came and went and I was grateful when we reached Peri's.

It had been agreed I'd stay in Peri's spare room, but getting out of the car I headed down to my flat.

'You can't go down there, it's a crime scene,' said the first officer.

'I want pants,' I said flatly, and he looked more confused than embarrassed. Peri took charge, guiding me into her flat, collecting my keys and then she disappeared with the police, to reappear minutes later with some pants. They were cotton and flowery and mine, and I burst into tears.

The police made arrangements with Peri to return the next day and left.

Tired, hungover, battered and in shock, I was lucky to have Peri. I'd gone to school with her daughter, with whom I'd shared the flat that I was now renting alone. I knew her to be a feminist (of the seventies kind)* and could take her outrage and empathy as read. A strange mix of steely and absent-minded, she was also intelligent, kind, and being both an American and a problem sleeper, had a

---

* Steph told me when a teenager that any reading material left in the bathroom by her or her brother would mysteriously vanish, and in its place, copies of the *New Internationalist* would appear. It was sneaky, Steph agreed, but it worked.

robust selection of sleeping pills. Temazepam seemed the way to go, and she gave me a 'jelly' and a huge hug, and showed me to her spare room.

I closed the curtain against the winter morning light and slowly undressed, pulled on my pants and crawled into bed. Following Peri's advice I bit down on the capsule rather than swallowing it (speeding up the absorption rate). It tasted vile, but was swift.

Chapter Two

*The thought of suicide is a great consolation –
with the help of it one has got through many
a bad night*

FRIEDRICH NIETZSCHE

I WOKE WITH A START. The room was strange, the smells unfamiliar – 'Where am I? What's going on? Ah, that's right, I'm at Peri's, I was attacked.' I could hear noises downstairs, footsteps and conversations. It was just after noon, five hours since I'd passed out.

'I don't want to wake her,' said Peri, while other voices apologized and demurred. When did she think I'd be up?

I just lay there, comfortably warm, comfortably safe. I was aware that I didn't think I was in too bad a shape. Rationally I was OK. I hadn't been killed – that was a plus. Neither were any limbs broken. I hadn't been stabbed. OK, so my eyesight was fuzzy, particularly my right eye, and my bloody skull hurt like billy-oh, but other than that, a narrow escape. At no point did I use the word 'rape'.

I suddenly burst into tears. What I thought and how I

felt seemed to have nothing to do with one another, which was scary. I hate crying at the best of times, and tried to collect myself, but even deep breathing and concentrating on a spot on the ceiling didn't help. I sobbed and sobbed and sobbed . . .

Then, as suddenly as it started it stopped, my breathing evened out and I sat up. A shocking pain shot through my sinuses causing me to curse. I could tell from the shift in the murmurings downstairs that I'd been heard. Footsteps then a gentle knock-knock.

'You awake?' Peri asked, not coming in. I asked her to come in.

'It's the police photographer – they need to record your injuries.'

Oh, great. Just what I want, to be looked at. She told me they could always come back later, but I said no – I had a show to go to. Peri looked concerned.

'Show?'

I told her it was the last two performances, matinee and evening, and then the set gets struck and everyone goes home. Both shows had sold out, and I *was* going to be there. There were goodbyes to be said and applause to listen to. Theatre isn't like TV, there are no repeats – when a show is done, it's done. I was going to be there. He wasn't taking that away from me. Peri had that look that mothers have when they're trying to be supportive, but remain unconvinced. I said I'd be down.

I washed and brushed my teeth, but figured smartening myself up would be defeating the purpose. The facial bruising was bad, but not too bad (I reckoned I could get through the show, passing it off as the result of a drunken accident). I remembered the arnica and Ibuprofen that Peri had given me, wondering whether it had worked, and if, in retrospect, taking it had been a good idea. It would look better if I looked worse.

The police photographer was chatting with the two nice policewomen I'd met last night, and they stopped talking as I descended the stairs, not ready for my close-up.

A cup of tea and some toast later, I balanced on Peri's strange leather-back chair while the photographer dipped and swerved, snapping away, his conversation reduced to 'chin up' and 'look left', 'eyes closed', which was disconcerting. Obviously I didn't expect him to say 'cheese' or 'give me warm', but usually we have some sort of social relationship with the person snapping us. It took me a few moments to understand that *I* was not being photographed, my *injuries* were – I wasn't the subject, I was the canvas.

But at least he was brief and as soon as he'd finished he was gone.

The policewomen asked me how I was, and whether now would be a good time to start on my statement. I said no, tomorrow, I had a show to go to. When I explained, they were a great deal more enthusiastic than Peri ('Don't let him get you down!') and we arranged for them to come back the following day.

Now it was time to get ready. Which was tricky. What

was I getting ready for? Being around people? What would I tell them? I'd already decided (without thinking about it) that this was not something cast and crew needed to know. But what about friends in the audience? And family. How was I going to tell them? In the days before email and text, there were few outlets available for dispersing information other than the phone (and only by speaking to someone in person, this wasn't something that could be left on a machine), meeting up or sending a letter. Either way, I was coming up against the first excruciating hurdle for any victim in a rape story.

You've been attacked, and now *you* have to take the responsibility to tell those who care about you, and then *you* have to deal with their distress at your distress. The temptation to pretend you're OK, to make them feel less awful so you don't have to deal with their reaction, is almost overwhelming.

Yet, paradoxically, at the same time I was aware that I didn't want to hide the offence. I wasn't ashamed, didn't feel the slightest bit guilty, and in the cold light of day didn't see why people should have real life ameliorated for them. In the face of such internal confusion, it becomes easier to just not deal with it. It's not quite denial, it's more a delaying tactic.

And so, having decided that this could wait, I grabbed my keys and headed downstairs to my flat – I needed my hair-dryer, make-up, clothes, and, of course, more pants.

*

I don't know why – habit I suppose – but I assumed my flat would be empty, and yelped on discovering it was now heaving with SOCOs (Scenes of Crime Officers). Unlike TV's *C.S.I.*s, these SOCOs didn't waft around in designer gear trading one-liners. They wore hair nets, white-paper bunny suits, big white-paper slippers, and sported the kind of cheerfulness you see in 1950s films.

'Mornin', love!' said the chief SOCO, bouncing to the door to stop me coming in any further. 'You can't come in without these.' He handed me some white-paper booties. 'Sorry.'

He mistook my expression. I said it wasn't the boots, I didn't expect to see so people in my flat.

'Sorry, but the sooner the better.'

Nobody asked my permission. I wouldn't be comfortable letting a close friend plough through my personal possessions, and yet there they were, half a dozen alien-looking people, digging around willy-nilly. Only of course there was nothing willy-nilly about it. They knew what they were looking for, and as with the photographer and my face, I quickly adjusted. This wasn't just my home, it was a crime scene. And these people were on my side.

Slipping on the booties, the SOCO chief gave me a whirlwind tour. ('Sorry about the mess – mind how you go – don't touch anything.')

His team smiled and said hello, and assured me if there was anything to find, they'd find it. Following their trail of silver fingerprint dust you could almost trace a kinetic pattern of the previous night's events. The door frames and door handles were being dusted, as was my briefcase, having been opened and its contents strewn on the floor and the case then tossed aside, and my phone and the severed cables. The knives were in sealed bags.

Making our way into the kitchen the head SOCO asked me whether I smoked Benson and Hedges. I replied no, Silk Cut. 'Ah-ha!' he said, and led me outside into the garden.

I finally understood what had happened.

Years earlier, Steph and I had tried to turn the back garden into a space where we could sit and have drinks on a summer's night. We put two chairs outside, but soon realized that sitting in the garden sipping white wine like a couple of sophisticates was never going to happen – it just wasn't us, plus, we weren't south-facing, and I don't get on with midges, so, like the art student and writer we were, within weeks we gave up.

But we only took in one chair – the other, broken and lacking a back, was simply abandoned, to be thrown out later.

The attacker (I refuse to call him 'my attacker' – we did not have a personal relationship – people don't say 'my mugger') had skipped over two walls to get from the street into my back garden, and then dragged the chair to the kitchen window. There, the head SOCO explained, he'd stood on it, and reached in through the slender window at the top (no more than sixteen inches by five), which allowed him to reach down and open one of the larger windows directly beneath it. Then he was in.

I remembered in grotesque detail how just before I turned in, I had one of those quick 'head' conversations. 'I've been smoking – should I open the top window? Yeah, the room needs airing,' closely followed by the associated reassurance, 'The window's tiny, no one can get in through there.'

I'd done it hundreds of times before, just as hundreds of times I'd concluded, 'No, it's too cold,' and shut it. It could have gone either way, but in the end, I flipped the window open, set it on its catch and let him in.

There was more. I'd been asked about B&H because they'd found a dozen or so fag butts scattered around the chair, which meant one thing. He'd waited for me to come home and go to bed – one cigarette at a time . . .

I still find the idea of being stalked, him waiting for my return, watching me get ready for bed utterly horrendous. It was and still is the source of most of my nightmares – not the attack, but being watched as a prelude to being attacked. It's left me with a long-lasting self-consciousness within my own home – like thinking Stalin is watching you. I'm still a curtain-closer. I don't like people looking in – not ever. If I could live on the top of a mountain with no properties facing me I would.

'Is that your chair?'

I nodded, distressed.

'It's not your fault, love,' he said.

'They're cunning, these bastards,' said the SOCO, dusting the chair.

I felt sick and stupid. If only I'd removed the chair, not

opened that window. If only, if only ... Queasy, I was led to the bedroom (not 'my' bedroom, 'the' bedroom), where the door was being dusted and the latest infra-red technology was being used to pinpoint the blood on the wall. They'd ringed the blood on the duvet too.

The SOCOs silently moved aside and let me in. My instinct was to get out of there as quickly as possible, so rather than sort through clothes for an outfit to match the occasion, I just grabbed some stuff and left. I thanked the SOCOs, who said a cheery 'bye' and 'see ya'. 'We'll soon be done!'

Despite Peri's reservations, I got a cab to the West End and made it through both shows, standing at the back of the stalls in a daze. Every now and again I would well up, and grapple for control. Everyone assumed my heightened emotional state was due to the show closing, which I admit rankled – I'd never get *that* upset about a damned show. But if I told them what happened I might break down, and that would never do.

I vaguely remember telling my agent I'd been attacked, which backfired on me later that evening when various people said how sorry they were to hear about the mugging. Apart from a couple of techs commenting on my facial bruises (I said I'd been drunk and walked into a door, and they laughed), nobody asked any awkward questions. I avoided friends in the audience, kept a tight lid on it and stumbled through my goodbyes. The only time I nearly lost it was in the cab home. The driver, well-intentioned, middle-class, ex-teacher, kept trying to interest me in renting his sister's house in France. 'It's in the South, has four rooms, two of them doubles, and it's right near the sea,' he babbled on.

I repeatedly said, 'No, thank you,' and, 'Please, I just want to sit quietly,' but he wouldn't stop. 'The local cafes are wonderful, the neighbours friendly,' and he went on to describe the interiors, the fittings, even showing me a photo when we stopped at a red light. When I said very slowly and pointedly, 'It's been a difficult night,' he replied briskly, 'That's why you need a holiday! Ha-ha,' and kept on going.

I genuinely believe I could have killed him.

'You can't blame me for trying!' he said brightly as I alighted.

'You're a good brother,' was the best I could muster as I paid him. It wasn't his fault.

Peri had gone to bed. I slowly closed the door, crept over to her sofa and collapsed. It was over. The show was finished, that chapter of my life done. I could stop now.

I doubled up and howled, squashing a cushion to my face so as not to disturb Peri. I was lost. Nothing I'd learned or understood to be true up to this point had prepared me for this. I can do stoicism, sarcasm, depression, outrage, self-righteousness – the emotional vocabulary of the unhappy middle-class.

But I lacked a language and a map to steer me through this misery. 'It's not fair' and 'What am I going to do now?' were the best I could come up with, as I cried, endless wracking sobs that I'd only seen on TV, when the actors are so into it they manage to drool. Despair is the only way I can describe it, and that still seems too literary a description. If I could have lain down and quietly died that night, not at my own hand, but at the hand of some invisible grace, I would not have complained.

I made my way to bed, chomped down on yet another of Peri's 'jellies' and passed out.

Chapter Three

To want to forget something is to think of it

FRENCH PROVERB

LIGHT BURSTING THROUGH the curtains. I again woke with a start, but this time I was surprised to find I felt better, in fact I felt absolutely zingingly great. I was a survivor after all, I just needed a few weeks' rest (I worked it out at six, for some reason), and then I'd start looking for a job. By the time DC Keely Smith and another WPC turned up to take my statement, I was genuinely bouncy.

Crammed into Peri's small kitchen, her cat scratching at the window trying to get in, Keely apologized for asking me to go through it again, and explained it was police procedure to ask victims to repeat their story in case some small detail or forgotten fact worms its way into your consciousness and gives them a lead. What happens though is the repetition reduces your experience to a dull sequence of events. This happened, and then this happened, and then after that, another thing . . . It's why all police statements read the same way – flat and in past simple, with no emotional through line.* If Byron was mugged it would still read, 'I walked down the road in a northerly direction and then . . .'

I never said I was 'terrified', and didn't record my relief when I realized he didn't have a knife. In fact, at no point in this four-page document is there any record of how I felt. Maybe it's unnecessary. Maybe it's taken as read. But reading it back, the only word that resonates as being unequivocally mine, and not 'police speak', is 'pottered'.

> *I heard the taxi pull away. The flat was in order and I pottered around and let myself unwind.*

Plodding on, we got to the black-man-asking-for-cigarettes-bit, and to quell and possible future argument, I made sure my statement read:

> *I got the impression the black boy did only want cigarettes and seemed genuinely pleased when I gave them to him.*

I even changed 'man' into 'boy' so there could be no mistake, and added 'he continued walking in the direction of Canonbury' so they knew he wasn't interested in me. When we took a break, it became clear that I was a popular victim down at the station. Keely had just worked

---

* Like the 'begat' bits in the Old Testament, or *Mein Kampf*, which vileness I tried to read once as a sociological exercise (it's six hundred and fifteen pages of 'And another thing').

on a case were a man had dragged a woman into an alley and forced her to perform oral sex, and Keely couldn't work out why the victim hadn't been more like me, and grabbed his 'you-know' (as she called it), or bitten it off.

Both assured me I'd done well, and that they'd have done what I'd have done. But I knew something the police didn't. I'm *not* brave.* I have always hated it when people called me brave, partly because I feel it implies women who don't fight back are somehow cowards, which completely misses the point, partly because I knew my survival had more to do with dumb luck than character – those few seconds where I played dead weren't strategy, I simply did the next thing that occurred to me. I can't be sure, if I'd found myself alone for whatever reason with a man who turned nasty whether I would have fought the way I did. The circumstances simplified it in that *he* started it, which might sound odd, but is an important distinction – I didn't initiate the violence and therefore wasn't so much fighting as resisting. I didn't have time to consider, 'If I punch him this might make it worse,' which has cowed me in many a previous threatening situation. The threat of violence is in many ways more terrifying than actual violence and I'm certain if menaced, slowly and deliberately, I could be subdued. Such is biology that even the puniest man has more fighting power than the strongest woman when it comes to unarmed combat – it's to do with muscle density. I

---

* And I'm not modest either. No, really, I think I'm great.

was very put out years before when having challenged my then boyfriend to an arm-wrestling competition (he being an incredibly sweet, non-violent accountant, me being an athletic, determined woman, who was also taller than him) he squished me in seconds. Add to that a propensity for viciousness, and there's no way a woman can take out a man, unless she's (a) been specifically trained, (b) armed, or (c) like me, gets lucky.

It was only years later, while reading memoirs of a Yugoslavian partisan during the Second World War, Milovan Djilas,* that I realized being cowed into submission isn't a feminine reaction, but a human one. Djilas gave his account of a massacre of unarmed prisoners.

There was a story that I'd slaughtered the Germans in hand to hand combat. Actually like most prisoners, the Germans were as if paralysed, and didn't defend themselves or try to flee.

Even soldiers subjected to years of political indoctrination and racial theories that cast them as uber-men, once overpowered and in a hopeless situation, lined up and had their throats slit like sheep. (The partisans didn't use guns because that would have alerted the nearby German army, yet still, none of these soldiers cried for help or made a dash for freedom. Hopelessness pacified them completely.) But this idea of 'what we'd do' permeates popular

* *Wartime* by Milovan Djilas (Harvest Books, 1980).

narratives. Action films and the like present us with dilemmas and crises, and invite us to imagine how we'd behave ('Run away!' 'Call the police!' 'Don't go in there!'), encouraging the belief that if you're quick, smart, brave and strong (like the hero) you'll be OK. Which is naivety wrapped up in nonsense. Nobody knows how they'll behave in any given situation until that situation arrives. It's a common trope in the military that you never know how soldiers will react to danger, until the battle starts.

I still find being called brave hard to handle, just as I dislike the distinction made between 'good' and 'not-so-good' victims. It crops up all the time in debates, where those of us who were attacked by strangers are perceived as greater victims and thus deserving of more respect and sympathy than those attacked by acquaintances, which not only plays us off against one another, but also reduces our experiences to reference points in some greater moral argument.

For what it's worth, my experience as a 'good' victim suggests to me that acquaintance rape isn't lesser, it's just different. I had to deal with the horrific consequences of a nameless attack, but at least I knew it wasn't personal. Apart from being tortured by my foolish decision to leave the window open, I wasn't wracked with guilt for not being wiser or more adept. I was spared knowing the identity of the man who attacked me, and could not be regarded as responsible, however tendentiously, for the assault. Plus I wasn't attacked by someone who was part of a greater social circle, where telling the truth would carry a whole new set of pitfalls and consequences. No one has ever suggested that I wanted it, or made it all up because I'm vicious, crazy or a repentant shag. Even when it comes to the fear, I'm not sure which is worse – a sudden attack, or the creeping sensation that something's going horribly wrong, and you're trapped. I have been spared any and all of these burdens.

The language is different too. 'Stranger rape' sounds a whole lot nastier than the misleading Americanism 'date-rape' – which implies the encounter was already headed in a romantic direction, and thus rape could be the result of gender misunderstanding, the man simply 'going too far'.*

You cannot 'misunderstand' a penis into a vagina – it necessitates a deliberate effort. Rape isn't the result of a breakdown in communications, it's a conscious act of will, by one party to subordinate and dominate another. Yet this nonsense is trotted out by the great and the good, most recently by Helen Mirren, who, in an interview with *GQ* magazine (which we should remind ourselves means *Gentleman's Quarterly*, in other words a magazine for men), revealed she had been 'date-raped' a 'couple of times'.

Despite conceding that what happened to her *was* rape,

---

* When the forensics team were kind enough to invite me to New Scotland Yard, to meet the man who found the fingerprint match, I was disturbed to hear the senior police officer who was escorting me tell me how difficult the police found it to distinguish between 'real rape cases' and those where the man had simply misunderstood and 'gone too far'.

Mirren said that if a woman ends up in bed with a man and says no to full sex, but is forced into it, 'I don't think she can have that man into court under those circumstances. I guess it is one of the many subtle parts of the men–women relationship that has to be negotiated and worked out between them.'

I've never heard rape called subtle before.

'It's such a tricky area, isn't it?' she continued 'Especially if there's no violence. I mean, look at Mike Tyson – I don't think he was a rapist.'*

Washington's testimony was supported by the hospital ER doctor who examined her and found 'abrasions consistent with forced or very hard intercourse', and the chauffeur who saw her afterwards testified she was 'dazed, disoriented . . . scared' and 'in a state of shock'.†

But this falsehood that if a woman doesn't emerge from a room with a broken nose then she hasn't really been attacked ('especially if there's no violence') persists. Dovetail that with the popular belief exemplified by Mirren that 'no one can ever really know what happens between a couple when they're alone', and it's no surprise that conviction rates in this country remain in single figures.

In the latter claim, too, the language is subtly loaded.

---

* Tyson was found guilty of raping Desiree Washington in 1992 and served three years.

† Tyson, when released from prison, said, 'I just hate her guts . . . Now I really do want to rape her,' and more recently in a documentary, *Tyson*, claimed: 'I may have took advantage of women before, but I never took advantage of her.' So he 'took advantage' – i.e. raped – other women, but not Washington. Well, that's all right, then.

Two people do not a couple make, and 'alone' suggests an intimate situation has been sought by both parties. Over the years many women have told me their rape stories, and none of them fit this pattern of 'date-rape'. All of them were raped by acquaintances, who (of those reported or later challenged) *claimed* it was a date and the sex consensual.

Even among my statistically insignificant sample, it was noticeable that three women, of different ages, who had been raped at different times and in different cities, had uncannily similar stories.

They'd all attended a social function (one wedding, one party, one work do). They were about to call a cab to go home. A man at the function asked where they lived, and when they told him said, 'It's on my way – do you want a lift?' and they said, 'Yes, thank you.' Once at hers, the man asked if he could nip in and use the loo as he was bursting, the women being polite and grateful for the lift, said of course. The man entered the flat, used the toilet, but when he came out, grabbed the women, and started kissing and fondling them aggressively. Two women were overpowered and 'gave in', as they put it, to avoid worse violence. One woman struggled and was told by the man, 'You'd better stop that, because I'm going to get what I came for.'

None of these victims reported their rape to the police because they felt there was no point. They'd been drinking, left a party with a man and then let him into their flat. The similarities in their cases suggest that rapists have scripts, as do conmen and burglars.

But the idea that rape is simply the result of changing sexual mores has led to the government producing guidelines to clarify these supposedly new 'tricky negotiations'. Yet even the idea that men need to ensure consent at every stage has been met with derision. Does this mean men have to constantly ask for permission during sex? they scoff.

Well, yes, that's exactly what it means. Sex isn't something one party 'does' to another, it's something two people do together. Reciprocity, with its requests and permissions – 'Do you like that?' 'Is that good?' 'Are you ready?' 'Enter slowly' or 'Not so hard' and for men 'Don't use your teeth!' – is considered normal when two people have sex, especially for the first time.

It's called foreplay.

(For the record, I've said no, while semi-naked, and in bed with a man. I was in my early twenties, we'd met at a party, had loads to drink and fell through the door snogging and up for it. So why did I say no? Because his cock wasn't clean. ['Eeeuw – that's not going anywhere near me,' were my exact words.] Did he rape me? No. Why? *Because he wasn't a rapist.* He admitted he hadn't had a shower in a couple of days because his boiler was broken. I offered to run him a bath, but to be honest, the moment had passed. He left disappointed and embarrassed, but it wasn't the end of the world. Also, less flatteringly, I've had a man leap from the bed mid-coitus because he thought he heard his car alarm go off. Sex does not have an unstoppable momentum.)

Even the intelligentsia can't stop themselves. When David Cesarani wrote his biography of Arthur Koestler,* in which he revealed that the Hungarian intellectual was a bully, a wife-batterer and a serial rapist, he was roundly attacked.

One of the women Koestler raped was the author and film-maker Jill Craigie (once married to former leader of the Labour Party Michael Foot). The novelist Frederic Raphael said in Koestler's defence that 'abuse of women was (if it is not still) a certificate of virility in many great men' and that Craigie 'may have been excited by the risks'. He summed up Craigie's rape thus: 'We need not doubt that force was used or that understandable shame explains why the facts have taken so long to come out. Without being ungallant, however, I was reminded of a judge who told me that the crucial questions in such cases were: "Did you bite him? Did you scratch him?"'

Once again, if a woman doesn't emerge from the room with a broken nose, then she hasn't really been attacked. After publication of Cesarani's biography, Craigie told how Koestler had abused her hospitality when she invited him to lunch, raping her while banging her head against the floor. 'I was very young and naive. I just thought he had gone mad. I never knew he could do such a thing. 'I remember sitting on my steps with my clothes torn for what seemed like hours.' 'This was all about power,' she said. 'I tried to forget about it.'

---

* *Arthur Koestler: The Homeless Mind* (Heinemann, 1998).

The writer Julian Barnes (also a friend of Koestler's) likewise pitched in, accusing Cesarani of 'moral prating' and saying of Jill Craigie's rape, 'I don't think she was making it up, I just think the details may have been a little less lurid than described.'

I'd love to hear his description of what constitutes a non-lurid rape. But such is the nonsense trotted out about acquaintance rape, that, paradoxical as it seems, I've often been grateful that I was attacked by a stranger.

So let's repeat the obvious, rape is rape. And I'm not brave, I'm lucky. But there I was – the perfect victim – eloquent, feisty, and everybody was on my side.

Chapter Four

Deep unspeakable suffering may well be called a
baptism, the initiation into a new state

GEORGE ELIOT

Monday

THE POLICE HAD arranged to collect me first thing to
take me to the station so that my fingerprints and shoe-
prints could be eliminated from enquiries. I again woke in
a state of near euphoria. I didn't realize (and there was no
one to advise me) that these strange bursts of euphoria were
the remaining shots of adrenaline pulsing through my system. Ask any soldier – there's nothing like nearly dying to
make you feel alive. Dennis Potter said after he was diag-
nosed with terminal cancer that the blossom on the trees
had never seemed so blossomy, and I knew what he meant.
Feeling alive, however, is not the same as feeling happy,
it's an overwhelmingly animal sensation. You can smell,
taste and see things with an intensity that makes you wonder what you've been missing, but these surges come
wrapped up in recklessness and bravado. You could jump
off a tall building, run through traffic with your eyes shut

and drink anything handed to you. Just for the hell of it. It's Baudelaire's breath of the wings of madness.

When Keely turned up she was excited too. The police had a lead, they thought, of sorts. That weekend, a further two women had been violently attacked, one sexually assaulted, the other raped, just ten minutes from my flat, in Finsbury Park. As these attacks happened outside, the police thinking was that having failed to rape me indoors, the rapist thought he'd try his luck outdoors.

I wasn't greatly reassured to hear that either the man who attacked me was rampant or there was another madman on the prowl, but reiterated that if it was the same man and he was caught, yes I'd press charges. I read and signed my typed-up statement, wincing at the horrible prose (which baffled Keely – 'It's a great statement,' she said. 'No, really, you should read some of them.'). And we headed for the station.

The fingerprinting was strictly old-school, squidgy black ink and a roller – fingers, thumbs and then the heels of my hands ('Does that ever come up?' I asked. 'Uh-huh,' said the man doing my dabs. 'Cheque fraud, people rest their hands on the counter.') On our return, my neighbour Martin, a regular visitor, bounded up, his usual chipper self.

'Abs, what's going on?'

He told me he'd asked the SOCOs and the police, but all they would say was that there'd been 'an incident'. The police went in with Peri while Martin and I sat on the front wall and shared a cigarette.

'I was attacked in my bedroom by some nutter.'

'Fuck me! No way!'

'Yeah, Friday night, it was bad.'

'Did he try and . . . you know?'

'Yeah, and he broke my nose – look.'

'Fucking animal. How'd he get in?'

'Through the kitchen window.'

'Fuckin' hell!'

And then into the gory details, punctuated by Martin's alliterative swearing. It was easy telling him and I learned a lesson. Those to whom bad things have happened intuitively get it. It's people who have cosy lives, nice families, money in the bank and loving relationships that are the problem. Martin and his girlfriend Kelly* grew up in care. Both knew that the world was not fair, and that although really bad shit doesn't happen often . . . it still happens. Later, when Martin of his own volition approached a police officer and offered to give his finger- and boot-prints for purposes of elimination, I was supremely touched. For a black man who'd 'got up to mischief' as he put it as a teen, Stoke Newington police station was not a place to idly visit.

Years later, on a train to Edinburgh, I was reading a book about post-traumatic stress disorder and the middle-aged Scouser sitting opposite apologized for interrupting, and asked if it was any good, and why I was reading it, was I a doctor? I fudged and said I'd been badly beaten

---

* Eighteen years and three kids later they're still together, and incredibly happy.

up some time ago, and was trying to understand PTSD. He said how sorry he was to hear I'd been hurt, and told me he'd had PTSD as a young man ('not that they called it that then'), and it still sneaked up on him on occasion. I asked him how he came to have it, and he told me.

He'd joined the British army at seventeen, which, like many a working-class lad, had been his only ambition. This being the 1970s, after basic training he was stationed outside Belfast in Northern Ireland.

Within weeks a car bomb went off in the city centre, causing multiple deaths, and he was detailed to collect the body parts scattered across the streets. With a shovel and a sack he got to work, becoming more and more distressed at the carnage. An elderly woman noticed him fighting back the tears, and patted him on the shoulder.

'Don't get upset, son,' she said sympathetically – 'they were only Catholics.'

He was, needless to say, Catholic himself.

I shared with him my story, and we discussed our experiences openly. If the past is another country, then trauma is a paradigm shift. The causes of our suffering could not be more different, but the effect it had had on our minds, bodies and lives was painfully similar, and despite our age and gender differences, we strangers were fellow travellers.

Jean Améry* wrote that those who have been tortured

---

* *At the Mind's Limits: Contemplations by a Survivor on Auschwitz and its Realities* (Indiana University Press, 1998); Christopher J. Einolf, 'The Fall and

will forever remain different because they can never un-know what man is capable of. It's why survivors find it difficult to connect with the un-traumatized world and share our suffering, even with those who are closest to us. You try to find a common reference point, but there is none.

That moment, sitting on the wall with Martin, I felt less alone than I had done for days.

The next few days were a blur, my moods either up, up and away, or slumped so badly I could barely move, eat or dress myself. My doctor prescribed me my own supply of sleeping pills – but only in packs of seven tablets 'to circumvent the risk of overdose', which was thoughtful if not exactly tactful.

He also arranged for me to see a series of consultants, whereupon my head was X-rayed, my eyes examined, and the results were not comforting. I needed an operation on nose and my right eye, but this being the early nineties, I was warned there'd be a long waiting list. ('How long?' 'Over three years.')

I was also referred to the psychiatric wing of the Homerton Hospital in Hackney for what I was told was an assessment. It was a Victorian rundown ruin of a hos-pital, and in the waiting room I sat across from an elderly man, who was muttering, dribbling and hitting himself repeatedly over the head with a copy of *Woman's Weekly* as nurses and staff passed by uninterestedly.

Rise of Torture: A Comparative and Historical Analysis', *Sociological Theory*, volume 25 issue 2, 22 May 2007.

I was eventually called in, and gave the doctor my referral letter. A large woman with a booming voice, she glanced at the details, misread its contents, then asked loudly, as she opened the window (we were on the ground floor, people were passing outside just feet from us), 'So . . . Tell me about your sexual problems . . .'

I said one word. 'No.'

Got up and left.

No one suggested specialized counselling. Or if they did I wasn't receptive to it.

I still hadn't told either family or my friends, and the dread of it was getting worse. My friends suspected something wasn't right, because they'd been calling and leaving messages about the show, and were concerned not to hear back from me. My most persistent pal Barb eventually phoned my agent, who reluctantly told her I 'was not in a good place'. She immediately drove over to see what was up and I told her. 'What has your family said?' she asked, and I admitted I couldn't face telling them.

'Would you like me to call them?' she said.

'Yes,' I replied and instantly felt lighter. God bless friends. While she phoned my brother I went to get booze and fags. It wasn't the little break I hoped it would be. There outside the newsagents, instead of 'New Parking Crisis' or 'Infant School Set To Close', the *Islington Gazette* had picked up on the police's idea that all three attacks that weekend were linked and had emblazoned SEX BEAST'S REIGN OF TERROR on its billboard.

I bought a copy, and never having read about myself in the third person before, it took a second to realize the '28-year-old professional woman' attacked in her basement was me. I was furious that these people were using my suffering (and others) to sell copy, and began writing letters in my head to the journalist (it was a woman) about how she'd feel if it had happened to her, while also noting I'd made it into the professional classes.*

I returned home and asked Barb how it had gone. She said my brother was shocked, and would tell my dad and sister, but he was put out he hadn't been told sooner and was receiving the news second-hand. The grievances were starting. I hadn't handled this well.

I showed Barb the newspaper. 'You can't stay here,' she said, 'you're coming with me.'

---

* Ten years earlier and it would've said 'park keeper'.

Chapter Five

Home isn't where our house is,
but wherever we are understood

CHRISTIAN MORGENSTERN

A TRADITIONAL TRAUMA STORY (or at least all those
that I've come across) involves some sort of going 'home'
and falling into the arms of mother, being looked after,
fed favourite meals and allowed to recuperate within the
safety of the nest.

Even if my mother had been alive that scenario
would've been problematic. She wasn't tactile and I've no
memory of her touching me, let alone hugging me, or
telling me she loved me. But then again, I have no
memory of her shouting at me, or telling me I was stupid
or useless or not wanted. When vexed, the worst she ever
did was roll her eyes and mutter, 'Addle-pated child,'
which I didn't mind because I liked the word 'addle-
pated'.*

I can't say whether we were close or not, because I'm

---

* From **addle** (*adj*) muddled, unable to think clearly (origin seventeenth
century) + **pate** (*n archaic*) a person's head (origin unknown Mid. English).

not sure what the word means. Once, when I was eleven, I returned home having spent the summer holidays with one of her friends, whose daughter was roughly the same age as me. As I got off the train, I noticed that elsewhere in the station multiple reunions were going on, with people squealing, hugging, kissing, occasionally running to meet one another with glee. I walked up to Mum and wondered what to do. I had a feeling I should do something to mark the occasion of my return after four weeks away. So I held out my hand, and she shook it. It seemed to do the trick, and we went home.

In later years, I've put her emotional reticence down to her public-school education and the Second World War. Not the war directly – no men in our family were killed, no houses were bombed. But she was sent to boarding school aged six (working-class children were evacuated, middle-class ones sent to school) in a green tweed uniform she hated unreservedly. ('I loathed it,' she told my grandmother. 'Nonsense,' said Granny, not missing a beat. 'You looked marvellous.')

Although it wasn't a regular topic for conversation, 'school and the war' was always there in the background, often as a lead-in for a salutary lesson. When pleading for more hot water than the regulation puddle in my bath, she told me of her return to school after the fall of France. On bath night the girls were puzzled to see that each tub in the communal bathroom suddenly had a black plumb line on it. Then they saw the reason – a gleaming new plaque on the wall bearing the legend:

The King only uses four inches of water in his bath.
Would <u>you</u> use more?

Even at six she thought the underlining of 'you' was hilarious, but the lesson was well learned. You really don't need more, she said, and in a hotel, years later, I watched her run herself a bath with only four inches – all so we didn't lose the Second World War. She saved wrapping paper, collected string and kept buttons in a box, soaked unused stamps off envelopes, and bought strange contraptions to get the last scrap of toothpaste out of the tube and compress leftover bits of soap into a new bar. Her sayings still haunt me. 'Neither a lender nor a borrower be.' 'A thing's only worth what someone else will pay for it.' 'You must cut your coat according to your cloth.' And, of course, 'Elbows off the table.' Life skills were important, so I was taught to sew, and shown how to drag a chair to the cooker when I was five, so I could fry an egg before going to school ('If you've got an egg in the house, you've got a meal'). Every time an ad comes on telling us to turn down the thermostat and put on a jumper, it's as if she's risen from the dead in advertising form.

Like a lot of the communication between grown-ups and children, the important stuff was between the lines. One of those was a girl called Anya. Only mentioned once, when I was twelve, Anya has haunted me as she haunted my mother, despite a description so bald I don't know what she looked like, only that she was Jewish, and that imperial catch-all of the day, 'foreign'. They were good friends and slept in adjoining beds in the dormitory and Mum said Anya spent the whole war either dreaming of Tyrone Power, or waiting waiting waiting for it all to be over so she could be with 'Momma and Poppa'.

Then, one day, with the end of the war in sight, the headmistress interrupted their history class and announced they were going to the cinema. The school en masse formed a series of 'crocodiles', linking hands, and were marched off to the local flea-pit. It was packed, everyone in the vicinity was there – word had got out, this was 'important'. There was standing at the back.

Until this point, all the wartime newsreels my mother had seen had been relentlessly resilient – wounded soldiers on their way back to Blighty puffing on Woodbines and giving the cameras the thumbs up, Churchill visiting the troops, Princesses Elizabeth and Margaret Rose doing their bit, even bombed-out cities and civilian death were viewed through the propaganda prism of 'we can take it'. It was, as my mother put it, a war without blood.

Then the lights went down and Richard Dimbleby's report from Bergen Belsen* – the first major concentration camp to be liberated by the Allies – started playing.

As the screen was filled with bulldozers shovelling emaciated corpses into pits – a tumbling mass of murder, Mum glanced at her friend.

'Anya knew she was never going to see Momma and Poppa again,' she said flatly.

---

* Anne Frank and her sister Margot died there in March 1945.

The film was followed by absolute stillness – usually most people made a dash for the exit before the national anthem started but not this time – 'No one moved or stood up, they just sat there in complete silence, no one knew what to say.' It was never brought up again. But it made sense of why, despite a liberal philosophy and lifetime of travel, she never went to Germany. 'You wouldn't know who you were shaking hands with,' she whispered, and just as big a sin for the English middle classes, 'You wouldn't want to be polite to "the wrong person".'

Thankfully her drive for the practical was tempered by a fine sense of humour. When I was a teen, we had a breakfast argument about newspaper-reading rights – I was reading it, she wanted it. I posited that, this being a democratic and liberal household (we were arguing over the *Guardian*, for heaven's sake), I had as much right as she did to read the newspaper. She considered my point, and said if I gave her the paper, she'd let me have the arts section. This seemed like a fair deal, so I handed her the paper, and she started reading. 'What about the arts pages?' I said indignantly. 'Ah,' she replied with a quiet smile, 'that was just a ruse . . .'

Best of all, she was interesting, and interested. Because she could read Latin, being dragged around churches was almost fun, and speaking two languages and working as a London tour guide meant she was a wonderful pointer-outer.

To this day, whenever I pass the restaurant on the

Strand where we had the last meal, as well as shuddering and remembering that night, I also think, 'Oh, look, if you cross the road, and walk two hundred yards down to the embankment you'll find the only statue in London of a camel.'*

Her dying suddenly of ovarian cancer when I was twenty-one meant I never got to have any meaningful adult conversations with her, else I would've asked her what my siblings and I had wondered quietly for years. Why on God's earth was she married to my father?

* The Imperial Camel Corps memorial in Victoria Embankment Gardens.

Chapter Six

Happy families are all alike; every unhappy
family is unhappy in its own way

LEO TOLSTOY

I WAS THE YOUNGEST of three children, preceded by a brother, Mark, who was five years older than me, and a sister, Harriet who was eight. All last-borns arrive in an environment where the social structures are already in place and the role of the weakest and most vulnerable is to fit in, not to ask questions. Of course everyone grows up thinking their family is normal, but all unhappy families can be spotted by their rules. Ours were typical:

RULE 1. WE DON'T HAVE ANY SECRETS
RULE 2. DON'T TELL ANYONE ABOUT OUR SECRETS
RULE 3. RULES 1 AND 2 DON'T EXIST.

There are secrets that we know we hold, and there are secrets that we deny. Most powerful are secrets that combine the two.

We grew up in a dilapidated Georgian house in a

working-class neighbourhood, the type of property that people whispered about in the eighties, saying, 'And it only cost twelve thousand in 1963.' Four storeys high with coal fires, a leaking roof and mice, it seemed to whisper, like the house in D. H. Lawrence's *The Rocking-Horse Winner*, 'There must be more money! There must be more money!' The block was built square around a Victorian orchard, and from the upstairs back windows you could map the year's progress in the apple and pear trees as they went from bare to blossom to fruit. Inside, all the carpets were remnants, the walls were layered with shelves and the shelves were filled with books, my mother seeking out weekly jumble sales and bringing them back by the basket-load.

The road was quiet enough so you could play ball, ride your bike and be sent out on errands (provided you didn't cross the big road). It certainly wasn't posh – the house next door was abandoned for years, hence the mice, and the only landmark was the Kentucky Fried Chicken on the corner, unless you counted the actor Brian Glover (who lived at the other end), or the Ms Hendersons – identical middle-aged twins who shared a house a few doors down from us. With bottle-blonde hair and black pointed spectacles, they wore the same outfit every day – pink and turquoise trench coats with a chihuahua stuffed down the front, their dark eyes and wet noses glistening like buttons. I often wondered if these furry cravats were happy, but they weren't fat, so they must have got some exercise (I imagined indoor chihuahua Olympics with disciplines like climbing the stairs, jumping on a sofa, scaling a chair). Then one day Turquoise Miss Henderson looked bereft and flat-chested – a dog-spaced gap where a silk scarf now was. Her chihuahua had been hit by a car ('How?' I asked) and she, Pink Miss Henderson and her dog mourned deeply, knowing it would never be the same again.

Two blocks down, an elderly Jewish watchmaker whose shop smelled of machine oil would let you watch him work if you were quiet, or would chat happily, pushing his optic glass up onto his forehead like a strange myopic third eye. We had Mr Gregory the butcher (who delivered in a 'Gregory's box'), a fishmonger and a fruit and veg stall, and until Idi Amin threw the Asians out of Uganda, no shopping on a Thursday afternoon.

Mr Gruber (who I named after the shopkeeper in *Paddington Bear*) was my special friend. Polish, with greying hair and thick glasses, he ran the local deli. Long before paedophile scares were common currency I'd pop around on my own and he'd bounce me on his knee, giving me little packets of Polish fudge and teaching me words like '*dobja*' (which means 'OK' and has come in useful in later years). Years later, when writing for the BBC, I returned to Shepherds Bush and in the newsagents bought a copy of the local *Gazette* and saw Mr Gruber on page two, looking exactly as I remembered him because they'd used an old photo. 'Fuck me!' I said slightly too loud because I was still in the shop. Outside, under 'Flying Ace Dies', I discovered dear kindly Mr Gruber was a World War Two Spitfire pilot, decorated for service during the Battle of Britain, who was shot down over France, made his way back to Britain via the French underground and reported for duty next day. Stalin made going home untenable, and he settled here leaving his family behind. I wondered if I'd reminded him of his children. I'd missed the funeral but was delighted to see the RAF had stepped up and given him the works – brass band playing the Polish national anthem, medals on his coffin, everything.

As far as I was concerned, the outside world was a benevolent place, without any obvious authority or ill-will. Inside, however, was a different matter altogether.

A friend of my sister's described our family as five separate planets without a sun. If that was true, then my father was Mars. A gargantuan prop-forward of a man he was born in Lower Hutt (Awakairangi) just outside Wellington in Zealand. He paid his way over to the Mother Country by subscribing to the *New Yorker*, copying the cartoons and selling them on to New Zealand newspapers as originals. After such a larcenous start, a career in advertising was bound to follow, and sure enough, once in London, he joined an advertising agency in Knightsbridge, where he met my mother, who had finished pointing at things, at least professionally, and was now a copywriter, penning the classic Windolene advert.

Apart from meeting at an agency, I have no idea what they had in common. They never even looked like a couple, and when out, walked yards apart. He didn't read books or like films or the theatre, and although a fine draftsman seemed to get no joy from art, never went to galleries or said, 'That's stunning,' or, 'I wish I had my camera.' He did listen to music and liked gardening, but when I was young, as far as I could see, his only obvious passion was rugby. Richard Turnbull, the High Commissioner of Aden in the late 1960s, once lamented to Denis Healey that the British Empire would be remembered for two things, 'Association Football and the term "fuck off"'.

He forgot about rugby, which for those who don't know is New Zealand's unofficial state religion. If pulling on the red jersey is an honour for a Welshman, pulling on the black one is close to ordination for a Kiwi, and like all boys Dad dreamed of being an All Black. He was a good player, fast and tough (so he said, and I believed him) and got closer than most with a try-out for the under-16s, but a trick knee did for him (he twisted it so badly it was never right again). But he never forgot the haka,* and would do it at the drop of a drink, and my earliest images are of him watching rugby poised on the sofa like a silverback gorilla, slapping his bulbous thighs, jumping up and shouting at the ref. He'd get up at 4 a.m. and listen to matches on long-wave radio, his tape-recorder propped up against the

---

* A traditional Maori war dance performed prior to internationals, to assert national identity and put the other side off.

speaker, and accumulated mounds of cassettes, individually labelled with match, date, scores, ready to be listened to again. And despite our house being officially against racism, and the stream of news from Soweto showing South African policemen gunning down black children like rabbits, he was not deterred from watching and recording every single match of the 1976 All Blacks tour of South Africa. You don't need guns and butter when you've got rugby.

I can still see him in his study, back to the door, shoulders hunched, the 'don't even think of coming in' vibe oozing under the door. The only thing it seemed to me that he and Mum had in common was a reluctance to talk about their families. He had a few tales about how in Lower Hutt they used the paper that came wrapped around satsumas as dunny paper and I know his father was turned down from the army because of his flat feet. (He joined the Home Guard, and one great day in 1942 his brigade was finally issued with a machine gun, and so promptly went up into the mountains en masse, dug a pit, chased wild pigs into it before machine-gunning them down and having the mother of all barbecues.)

There were no Christmas cards, no presents, phone calls, nothing. The most descriptive thing he ever said about his family was that he had one brother who was 'all right', and another who was 'a peasant'. I didn't enquire further, but it was bad blood for sure. Other than that he came with no hinterland – all so-called family friends were Mum's friends and he just was what he was.

Up to the age of three I can safely say I adored him.

He was big and scary, but he was not mean, and when he put me to bed he'd read me a story and do all the voices. But when I was about three and a half it became clear that the house was full of rules, and breaking them was bad. Take not eating cat food. That might seem obvious, but our cat Hillary (named after Edmund Hillary) seemed to love it, and I loved Hillary. Tasting it seemed a normal thing to do, and to my unrefined palate it was delicious – pink, fishy and full of those crunchy calcified fish bones like you get in tinned pilchards.

I could tell by the way he said, 'Have you been eating cat food?' that eating cat food was a cross-maker, and said no. He sniffed my breath. I was a liar, *and* I had been eating cat food. Rather than dissuade me from eating compacted fish slurry, he got a tin and gave me a fork, towered over me and told me to start eating. This confused me, because, as I think we've established, I liked cat food. When I was in danger of finishing the tin, he grabbed it back and was about to lose his temper when we both heard a key in the lock, and froze. Mum called hello.

'Don't tell your mother about the cat food,' he said, and carried on as normal. I wasn't sure *what* I wasn't meant to mention. My eating cat food (which I wouldn't have brought up, knowing it to be bad) or him making me eat cat food. Later Mum noticed the food was missing.

'This tin was nearly full – have you fed the cats?'

'No,' he replied and threw me a glance. 'Maybe Harriet did.'

While she wondered, I realized two things. Children's

lies are bad, adults' lies are not bad, and the real mistake is getting caught.

Mark got caught when he was about eight. He slipped climbing the tree at the front that we weren't meant to climb, but with long sturdy branches mere feet from an upstairs window, it made squeezing out and clambering down just too tempting. His skull bounced off the fence post as he fell, and from where I was standing (safely to one side) I could see a chunk of scalp flapping in the breeze like a loose yarmulke. He was wobbling to his feet when Dad hearing the commotion appeared screaming and swearing. Then like a hurricane he disappeared, reappearing with a ten-pound sledgehammer that he'd grabbed from the shed, which he thrust into Mark's hands and started screaming at him to *PUT-THE-BLOODY-FENCE-BACK-UP-YOU-STUPID-BOY-I'VE-WARNED-YOU.*

I was only four and even I'd have called the ambulance (I'm not sure Mark ever saw a doctor). It's not remarkable, and certainly not blameworthy, to note that after this Mark became violent towards me. It's in the nature of things. Pain always goes downwards not up – there's never been a revolution where the rich have demanded the right to live in slums and work like dogs, chanting, 'What do we want? Dysentery. When do we want it? Now!' Like our father, Mark wasn't aggressive all the time, but once he discovered that he could hit me and get away with it, it became a regular occurrence.

Seeing an eight-year-old screamed at while staggering

around with a sledgehammer taught me another lesson. Everything belonged to Dad, even the garden fence.

Children understand possession, it's why you have to talk them into sharing toys ('It's twice the fun!' ''S mine'), but as children grow older they learn most houses have communal property. But not ours. In our house, even the TV was his and you had to ask permission to use it. He'd race in from dinner parties or trips to the cinema, and before taking off his coat, run upstairs to touch the set to see if it was warm and had been watched without consent.

Catching you out was a favourite pastime.

His study was next to the toilet and he would listen to check how much toilet paper you used (five pieces was enough). There were limits to the amount of butter you could use on toast, and once I asked to borrow a pencil. 'For how long?' he said. 'About an hour?' I shrugged, and he handed the pencil over. When I took it back, he checked his watch and gave me a nod. He almost had me, but no, I'd made it.

Once Harriet hit sixteen, he and Mum would go on holiday at least once a year, leaving us with an envelope full of cash and a list of instructions. Those two weeks spent eating sweets, watching TV with the central heating on, were the happiest of our year. But the first time they left, we discovered the hi-fi didn't work. Funny, worked the day before, Dad was listening to rugby. Took us a while to work out he'd removed the fuse. So we put the fuse in, used it, took the fuse out. Next time he went away, he made a diagram of where each dial was, treble, bass, volume, etc. . . . . even the numbers on the tape deck. That meant we had to copy down the dials and put them back to the right place. When he got back he knew we'd been using it, but couldn't prove it. We knew that he knew. And he knew that we knew that he knew. It was almost fun. And that was just for the hi-fi – there were rules covering everything.

Sometimes he'd just be mean for mean's sake, say, allowing you to watch the first five parts of a series on TV, then not allowing you to watch the last episode, because 'you slammed the door last Wednesday' or whatever, but you knew it was just because he could. So you adjusted, you didn't bring friends home – you went to theirs. You didn't care that your parents weren't there for sports day, nativity plays or whatever, you were pleased.

I realized very early on that his behaviour had nothing to do with mine; it wasn't cause and effect . . . If he returned in a bad mood somebody was going to get it. I learned to avoid him. Sitting in the kitchen, I could tell from the slam of the front door how he was feeling, and if it sounded bad I'd double back through the dining room, under the big table and shoot up the stairs.

He rarely came into my room because it was on the top floor, unlike Mark, whose room was next to mine. Blond and blue eyed, he looked so different from the rest of our family he could have been the fallout from an affair had not our Great-Uncle Alan looked the same. He passed through the same comprehensive I did but barely touched the sides, and although intellectually clever, and never bullied, made few friends; as Lisa Simpson wailed, 'I get straight A's *and* I'm a hall monitor, *why aren't I more popular?*' He was lumbered with the role of Good Son, and the Clever One,* and Dad's bullying seemed designed to destroy his masculinity – like encouraging him to play sports and then flattening him ('Old bull, young bull,' as Mark would say), but I rarely saw him bullied, merely felt it passed along. Probably as a consequence Mark was drawn to all things military. Lovingly painted Airfix models of Second World War fighter planes dangled from his ceiling like birds on a wire, and a keen Scout (it came with a uniform) he liked rules, or more to the point, he liked enforcing them.

I was wary of him. Like Dad he was inconsistent. You'd try not to get drawn into card games because three bad hands and he'd sulk or get vicious – so much resentment and anger and so few outlets. Certainly not the violin, which he laboured away at for years, before a departing music teacher said, 'Whatever you do, don't give up,' and it occurred to him that he could. (Sleeping next door, I was truly grateful.) On the rare occasions that we had guests, he was wheeled out as the one most likely to succeed.

I could draw up a dreary list of times Dad bullied me, but it always felt worse watching Harriet get it because she cared so much, and you felt like a coward, dying those thousand deaths each time you watched her picked on

---

* Harriet was the weak one, I was the flake.

and said nothing. It was disproportionately overt and deliberate, and I was much older before I understood why.

I thought she was glamorous, and with a big poster of David Essex above her fireplace, and Motown on the go, the cool one. She could dance up a storm, and loved Gene Kelly – his swaggering blue-collar acrobatics spoke to her, and she had a crush on him for years. But after years of dance lessons she broke her ankles jumping onto sand on a beach in Ireland that deceptively looked soft, but had actually set like concrete. The recoil snapped the bones, ominously beginning a perceived pattern of 'nothing goes right for me'.

Inheriting Dad's artistic bent she had a keen eye and dextrous hands, and her cat sculpture (made out of wire and papier-mâché) stood on a window ledge for years, always looking as if it might suddenly jump down, snaffling food on the way. Inheriting our father's shoulders too, she was an even better swimmer and was Middlesex champion in her teens. With soft brown eyes and red-brown hair (red from henna) she looked like a ingénue from a forties film. She was incapable of being unpleasant, and my only childhood grievance with her was film-related. Tasked by Mum to take me to the cinema during the school holidays, she took me to *The Sound of Music* six weeks in a row because she fancied the Austrian boy who joined the Hitler Youth and made me lie about having seen *Herbie* etc. . . . Other than that she was kind, and generous, and I was puzzled by Dad's reaction to her. He never praised her and once she hit thirteen/fourteen her very presence seemed to rankle him. He'd sniff contemptuously if she talked at the dinner table, then cut across her, stopping any interaction, sending out a clear message, she *wasn't* to be talked to. One Christmas after she'd left school and was working as a telephone operator – not a highly paid job – she was sixteen – she set aside money each week to buy a bottle of wine* so by the time it was Christmas she'd have a whole box. She researched the wine, wrapped each bottle, put ribbons and labels on them and stuck it under the tree in anticipation. On Christmas Day the grand moment came. He unwrapped one bottle, put on his glasses and read the label. 'Thank you, Harriet,' he said, 'very acceptable.' And that was as good as it got. She spent Christmas crying in her bedroom and I hated him for it. It was so calculated. All she wanted was for him to be nice to her. We never asked why Mum didn't intervene. We assumed she was OK with it, and to us, however unpleasant, it was normal.

A few years later Harriet had a complete nervous breakdown. She was meant to be looking after me while Mum and Dad were on holiday, and came home from work dizzy and excited, dragging bags of stuff that she'd bought, and a huge bottle – and I mean those two-footers – of champagne. Laughing and twirling around the flat like in her dancing days, she got drunker and drunker, and

---

* Like a lot of drunks, he fancied himself a wine buff.

happier and happier, before taking up residence in their double bed (which was very prohibited) clutching the bottle like a babe in arms, saying she wanted to tell me all about herself, and know all about me, and we stayed up all night talking. I thought she was acting out of character, especially when she told me she was Jesus and that Michael Aspel was sending her messages through the TV, but I went to school the next day and told a friend I'd had the best conversation with a member of my family that I'd ever had. When I got home that afternoon I found out she'd been sectioned.

She spent nine months in hospital, but really enjoyed it. 'If you're going to go mad, do it in south-west London,' she said, 'so they'll send you to Springfield.' Springfield, the mental hospital, had beautiful grounds and trees, and apart from the kerfuffle when it was discovered nurses had been using patients to grow cannabis in the greenhouses as part of their occupational therapy, Harriet looked back on her time there with affection.

After my parents returned from holiday, it became a non-subject. Every now and again, Mum would say, 'I've been to hospital,' and report back in the manner of a postcard: 'She seems to be doing well,' or 'The doctors are hopeful.' Years later Harriet told me she'd actually cried, 'What did I do wrong? What did I do wrong?' when visiting her. ('You married our father,' was my reaction.) They never took me to see her, and I never asked.

Call it Stockholm syndrome, call it what you will, as adults, my siblings and I had grown up to be stiflingly not close – meaning we spent more time in each other's company than most siblings, but avoided talking about anything real.

Despite my brother's lingering annoyance at being kept out of the loop, neither he nor my sister suggested I return to the family home. They knew why I wouldn't want to be around Dad. But it was never mentioned. Why break the habit of a lifetime?

Chapter Seven

We all boil at different degrees

RALPH WALDO EMERSON

WHILE THE NEWS was disseminated, I packed some clothes into a bin liner, thanked Peri and decamped to Barb's. There, like an invalid, I received guests (vetted by Barb) and spent a lot of time eating soup and telling people I was OK. My moods came and went, and my energy was displaced – sometimes I'd feel like sprinting till I dropped, other times I'd be crossing a room and realize I hadn't actually moved for ten minutes.

After a few days at hers I was desperate to come 'home'. I wasn't comfortable on her futon, and she was a singer so never put the central heating on and it was January, and I freeze if it's under seventy degrees, but complaining would be churlish.

I didn't want to be in my flat, but I wanted to be warm and near my things. And having been abused by some men at the market in Pimlico ('What a dog!' they yelled at my bedraggled form from a passing car), the outside world seemed no less hostile in South London than in North, so I returned to Peri's.

Tucked away in her spare room, we developed a friendly flat-sharing routine, eating our evening meals together while watching the *Channel 4 News*, talking about imperialism, misogyny, racism, even Islamophobia (Peri was half-Iranian), which I found relaxing.

Then came Bosnia. The war had been unfolding in the months before I was attacked, and now, day after day, the screens were filled with women who'd been raped, draped in shabby coats and baggy cardigans, their eyes lowered beneath their headscarves. It was all there to see. The brooding poverty of the Balkans, the ineffectualness of the UN whose small army of blue helmets was committed to be there but committed to do nothing but watch, as I watched too – these far-away women of whom I knew nothing, trapped between hopelessness and despair. Only Martin Bell, the man in white, seemed to give a damn.

I've noticed that the historical existence of rape in war is frequently used in argument by those who seek to absolve the modern media of any responsibility for creating the conditions for sexual violence,* as if there were no narratives before TV and the Web. They didn't have set-tops, but they had propaganda. To bowdlerize Voltaire – if you can get people to believe the ridiculous, you can get them to kill, and where people are killed, women are raped.

Downstairs, the crime-scene tape had long since been

---

* Similarly the phrase 'the oldest profession' is offered as evidence that prostitution is so old it must be in the nature of things rather than evidence that women have been poor, abused and exploited for millennia.

removed, and finally my phone was due to be reconnected.

'What happened?' said the white BT man laying the new cables, and, as this wasn't a personal relationship, I told him the blunt truth. I'd been attacked by a rapist.

'Black guy, was it?' he said, merely the first of many.

My black friends admitted they were relieved he was white, and then that they were embarrassed they were relieved (Peri as a lefty was embarrassed she was relieved). But everyone wanted to know and I became an expert at sussing out when they'd ask, and how euphemistically. 'Did you get a good look at him?' was popular, as was 'Can you describe him?'

I noticed that nobody ever assumed that he was white.

Despite Peri having told me I could stay as long as I liked, I grew weary of not having my own space. I was in a nether-world – not the practical world of working and living, nor the relaxed world of holiday. I couldn't face finding a new flat (in the stress stakes that's up there with death and divorce), and having nowhere to go, I prepared to move back into my flat. Friends were concerned, but I brushed that aside. Practicalities left no room for misgivings. I needed a front door of my own, and this was the only one available.

I dressed it up in defiance. 'He's not throwing me out of my home,' I declared. 'I won't let him beat me.' And so – after settling the back rent – I returned.

My family generously pitched in. Dad bought me a rape alarm and a new duvet cover (the one the police took with blood on it was never returned), and a friend of my brother's fixed metal grilles, now commonplace in basement flats, on all the windows.

I abandoned the bedroom, declaring it my new office, and dragged the bed into the front room, so that when I went to sleep I was behind a minimum of two sets of locked doors. I didn't care if I burnt to death, as long as I burnt to death alone. Strangely I left the fingerprint dust. Even at the time I wasn't sure why, it wasn't like it added to the decor. Maybe I needed a physical record of what had happened: 'See that around the window – I didn't make it up.'

It's easy to see with the benefit of hindsight that moving back in was perhaps not the most sensible course of action, but I needed the familiar, even if the familiar came at a price. Although not quite OCD, I veer towards the picky, and like doing certain things certain ways. For instance, I have to see movies through to the end of the credits, even if I've hated the film, which drives my friends insane. I can't pretend it's because I need to know that no animals were harmed during the making of the film, or that the characters bore no relation to persons living or dead, or that Kodachrome provided the film stock. It's simply the viewing has a beginning and a middle and an end. Now we can go. I'll happily order the same thing in the same restaurant and feel a quiet sense of comfort when it arrives exactly as described. I like Philip Glass and Bach because their rhythmic patterns are mathematically perfect, and when buildings are knocked down and new ones put in their place I inwardly grumble because it feels discordant.

Moving back in, although more a result of circumstance than choice, did at least allow me a semblance of control, and compared to women in Bosnia, returning to an unbombed-out flat, in a nice part of town and with good neighbours and a benign police force, might not have been perfect, but it wasn't that bad.

Before the big day, I spent a week treating the place as an office, commuting downstairs during the day then slipping upstairs to sleep. By now, the flat was the kind of winter cold that happens when the central heating's been off and the bricks have turned chill. It was days before I could wear less than three layers of clothing even with the thermostat on full.

The day before the 'day', a friend asked if I wanted the number of a spiritual 'healer' who could cleanse the flat of any lingering bad energy. Now, show me a foxhole and I'll be your atheist, but I wasn't averse to the idea that spaces hold memories. Once, when visiting a castle in Denmark, I walked into a stone room and was overcome by claustrophobia and panic. It wasn't a dungeon and there were no nasty implements around so my response seemed a tad extreme. I found the owner and, after praising his castle, questioned him about the room. 'Ah,' he said, 'that place.' He told me that in the eighteenth century a man was suspected of sleeping with the noble's wife. Because he was a man of position, he couldn't be executed, so the noble had him locked in the room. However, being a sadist, the noble then employed masons to construct an inner wall that ran diagonally across it. Every year, he had the wall moved forward a foot, until eventually the prisoner was living in two feet of space and went mad.

Bearing that in mind, getting rid of 'bad energies' seemed worth a punt.

The healer, Wendy, was shorter and posher than I'd expected, more like a member of the Women's Institute, or an extra on *Midsomer Murders* than a shaman (unless shamans wear brogues). Nevertheless, she had the hush about her of someone who took their work seriously, and set to, waving bunches of sage around and standing thoughtfully in each room, lighting the odd candle. It took a good hour, but job done, she was ready to go, and I thanked her and gave her forty pounds.

'I also removed the stabbing in the kitchen,' she said.

'I was attacked in the bedroom,' I said.

'I know,' she said. 'Previous occupant.'

I wasn't sure whether that qualified for a tip. After she left I went from room to room, and conceded the place did feel lighter and cleaner, or at the very least smelt nicely of stuffing, and I felt a lot better about moving in.

The night arrived and I checked and rechecked all the windows, locked my front door – then the hall door.

Then the back door, then the door in the corridor between the bathroom and the kitchen.

With the phone going every ten minutes with friends checking on me I felt cared for, and listening to music made me realize how much I'd missed it. Just before turning in I called 999 with the intention of hanging up before they answered, so the number was there as 'redial' (i.e., I only had to press one button not three should I need help). I was thrown when a woman answered, 'Police-fire-brigade-ambulance-which-service-do-you-require?' and slammed the receiver down. A minute or so later I picked it up to make sure the line was working. 'Hello?' said the woman's voice. 'Are you all right?' She said they never allow a line to go dead – just in case. I explained to her what I'd been trying to do, and she very kindly wished me a good night's sleep.

And so I knocked back a tablet (zopiclone, different from temazepam) and crawled into bed to sleep, perchance to dream.

The trouble with shock is that, like any other mental condition, it isn't evident to the naked eye, and unlike broken bones and bruises, doesn't heal with time. When we commonly say 'I was shocked' we mean we were surprised or aghast, and the word emphasizes our reaction in the moment. Traumatic shock is completely different. The feeling isn't just in the moment, its effects ripple outwards causing what I can only describe as a disjunction with reality. As far as the brain is concerned, the shocking thing about being attacked is not how violent it was, it's that it happened at all.

Soldiers know they might get killed. When we board a plane we know there's a chance it could crash. When smoking or drinking or cutting through an alley we know we're taking calculated risks, which is why we insist on safety measures.

There's no calculated risk in going to bed. No part of your brain is attuned to the possibility that you could go to bed alone in your own flat and wake up with a violent stranger. Furthermore, if you're unlucky enough to be shot, mugged or develop an illness, you can always leave the army, avoid alleyways, stop drinking. You can't not go to bed – and therein lies the problem.

Part of you knows that with the new locks, bolts and grilles you've taken the right measures, and it's not going to happen again. But you know it could happen again, because it shouldn't have happened in the first place. There's no natural place in this loop for your mind to stop because you've jumped from a cosy Newtonian universe of cause and effect where everything makes sense to a multiverse of utter chaos, where God is not just playing dice with the universe, he's opened a casino, where anything can happen to anybody, anywhere.

The first night I slept fitfully, which was only to be expected, but I felt a surge of relief at waking up in my own space with everything sounding right, from passing cars in the street to the gurgle of the water pipes.

My approach to sleep from then on was to find the right balance between official drugs and alcohol so that I sparked out the moment my head hit the pillow, and yet was not so under that I would be deaf to trouble. It didn't occur to me that anaesthetizing myself might have long-term consequences. I wasn't strategizing, I was dealing with problems as they came up, and for now, sleep was dealt with. Well, -ish.

During the day, traumatic shock presented a new range of reality distortions, coupled with a lingering sense of fragmentation.

To all intents normal to the outside world, I nevertheless found myself, like Schrödinger's cat, capable of being both OK and not OK *simultaneously* depending on how my attention was turned. I could be standing on a platform thinking, 'I hope the train comes soon, I don't want to be late,' while at the same time pondering, 'If I walk forward two yards onto the tracks everything will stop,' with neither thought coming in louder or more insistent than the other.

Familiarity carried me through the motions of wellness and I went to meetings, discussed work, spoke to my accountant, all the time willing and wanting to be 'fine', and of course, people mirror back to you the message you send: you're doing great – well done!

What you don't tell people is that you can hear what you're going to say before you say it – like déjà vu or a two-second transatlantic delay. The murmurs of disquiet began to pile up like last year's accounts and concentration was an early casualty. I would regularly lapse into 'Where was I?' which was a mask for 'How am I?' or even 'Who am I?' and would often just stare into the middle distance like a cat watching a card trick.

I completely understand people who say they're going to the shops and then disappear, leaving in their wake stunned friends and family who agree that they seemed perfectly fine – 'I chatted to them only yesterday . . .' When you're fragmented, it's easier to abandon one reality and set off to find a new one than try to integrate the current realities.

If it's true that trauma, like sport, or war, doesn't make character, it reveals it, then the hardest thing I had to accept was how fragile my personality was. I'm always surprised when people describe themselves – 'I'm hard but fair' or 'I don't suffer fools gladly' – when it's so clear it's not actually who they are, it's how they'd like to be seen.

I would've described myself as plucky and good-humoured, and, like members of my family and passive-aggressives everywhere, seen my major flaw as being 'too nice'. Now I was leaking emotional colours I assumed were others' – petulance, scorn, self-centredness, rage. If you've lived in a bubble of moral superiority (like me), when it bursts you realize not only how imperfect you are now, but also how self-delusional you were then. It's lose–lose.

Most frightening of all, my memory was starting to fail, and the alcohol wasn't helping – booze lines up your brain cells and shoots them dead centre. I was forgetting things I knew I knew, and failing to remember things I needed. I liked having a good memory – I assumed it was compensation for not being able to spell – and the world felt safer if you could tie down the past, not literally, of course, but if you remembered it accurately, it'd be there for later. I'm sure most people can remember the names of their classmates, and their first home phone number and maybe the number plates of parents' cars (grey Triumph Herald 969 AUW). I'd log furniture, paintings, where the light sources came into a room, incidents, conversations, meals. I'd borrow Tony Hancock records from the library and play them over and over until I knew them by heart. And why wouldn't you want to remember every Vice-President of the USA back to Alben Barkley? Or that Spiro Agnew is an anagram for Grow A Penis. Or that Ian Gillard played No. 3 for QPR for sixteen years. If I found something interesting, funny or just elegantly written I was in the habit of memorizing it, so I'd have something to think about in queues or waiting for a bus.

It was essential for work. Memory gives ideas context, allowing you to juxtapose and abstract and make sparks of connection. But now it was like rubbing two sponges together. Conversation would grind to a halt amid 'Oh, you know, what's-is-name' and 'What was that film called – that other woman was in it, the one with the brown hair, she starred with . . . oh, what's her name again . . .' You'd remember that a film had a funny scene, but couldn't remember the scene. It was like stumbling around in a dark attic.

Previously, I'd divided my writing time into two blocks, the evening for coming up with ideas, the day for writing them up. Now, as if applying for a place in my attention, my lower right arm started flapping. Not my whole arm, but from my elbow right down to the fingertips; with my hand splayed, my forearm twitched mechanically. Once noticed it was controllable – just – but alone and indoors, I didn't see the point, because it felt good. The rest of my body relaxed completely. I told myself lots of people twitch their foot when they're uneasy or bored and this was no different. It goes without saying that I didn't mention it to anyone.*

When news came through that the musical had been nominated for an award I thought maybe work might magically appear. But the show was dead, I wasn't invited to the ceremony and nobody seemed to need a musical-book writer. Maybe if I'd been a poet, or a proper playwright, I'd have been able to turn what was going on in my head to my advantage. But I did light ent, and there wasn't much light ent to hand.

So I did what all my family did.

---

* Writing this has seen the twitch return. It's as comforting now as it was then.

Chapter Eight

'Here's a rule I recommend: never practice
two vices at once.'

TALLULAH BANKHEAD

THERE'S NOT MUCH illuminating anyone can say about
the process of drinking because the results are so predict-
able. If Einstein drank two bottles of red, some brandy
and a beer, he'd talk shit, fall over and throw up like
everyone else. In fact the only remarkable thing about
drinking is how unremarkable it is – it's why all 'we got
caned at the weekend' tales are dull. ('And then Billy,
right, Billy threw up over this car, and the owner, right,
yeah the owner, he got so mad that he smacked him' and
so on and so on. I've yet to hear a drunkalogue that ends,
'When I came to, I was amazed to discover I'd written an
incisive short story!')

I was aware of drinking at an early age. It was something my father wanted to do, and my mother wanted to
stop. Because my sister was the first to reach adulthood
(she left school at sixteen), she was also the first to start
drinking (and smoke cigarettes first too). Martini was her

79

tipple, and then Blackthorn Dry cider. My brother was fairly abstemious before he went to Oxford, but came home a great deal more relaxed about most things, and always seemed happier after a pint or two of decent beer and a spliff.

Personally I only ever found two alcoholic beverages undrinkable, one, a vodka with caraway seeds in it, which was a waste of vodka, and I don't like vodka, and Gammel Dansk, one of those bitter liquors made by monks for over three hundred years but still tastes like crap.* You're meant to drink it in the morning before hunting, presumably to get you so angry you'll shoot things.

Getting drunk as often as possible is a teenage rite of passage, but there were always a few in our gang who liked it more, and I was one of them. Occasionally pubs were a problem, but no one really cared if teenagers got hold of drink, and you could get it everywhere. Before the drinks industry targeted the young with alcopops we were adept at adding blackcurrant to beer, and cream to liquor. Around fourteen years old poppers and dope drifted around the odd party, and everyone tried nutmeg and banana skins, but booze was without doubt king. Even if done recklessly, the drinking was convivial and fun.

In my twenties, despite never having been a student, I lived the student life with Steph, and we went to pubs,

---

* The label says, 'Gør godt om morgenen, efter dagens dont, under jagten, på fisketuren, eller som aperitif', which means, 'Gammel Dansk does you good in the morning, after the day's work, when you go hunting, on a fishing trip, or as an aperitif.'

played pool, and on a sunny day could be caught playing Beerhunter in the garden.* For a long minute it worked. The social phobia and unease I carried inside me was replaced by an upbeat confidence. I was writing by then, and most of my friends were comics and actors and writers and musicians and we all did pretty much the same.

But this time the drinking was frenzied, yet mundane. I didn't go to clubs, or get wasted at parties and behave outrageously. I repeatedly got just too drunk while out with friends, and when alone stumbled around the flat, letting baths overflow, bumping into doorframes, getting impotently angry.

He attacked me *because of my gender*. That was the criterion, you fucking evil piece of shit? How dare you? You didn't even know me.† All those movies where the hitman says, 'It's not personal.' That makes it worse. As far as I was concerned this wasn't a sex crime, it was a hate crime, and I hated him right back.

I replayed fantasies where I was a female version of RoboCop, strong, powerful, armed and supremely violent – everything I wasn't in real life. In my mind's eye, I'd find this man, and kill him, but not quickly, oh no. First I'd take out his knees, till he was sprawled screaming in his

---

* Take a six pack, shake one, put it back, then you each pick a can blindfold and open it by your temple until one goes off.

† I know that's close to being horrified when an OAP is mugged 'for only fifteen quid' as if there was an amount at which it would be OK. ('Eight hundred quid?' – 'Well, fair enough.')

own blood. Then I'd tower over him and Kapow! take off each arm, then when he was nothing but a squirming screaming torso I'd shoot him between his legs. Then, and only then, I'd kill him. But he'd have to ask. It was cartoonish, simplistic and highly unimaginative. No sooner would I have reached the fantasy's climax than I'd run it again. And again. Sometimes it changed, sometimes he begged and pleaded. Other times he taunted me, challenging me to do my worst. I always managed to do my worst. People often say figuratively, 'I could kill him.' I know I could kill, it's one of the things I've learned about myself, one of those shocks to my sense of self. I have no inclination to be conciliatory, and huge inclination for revenge.

By summer, the pace of descent was accelerating. Adding to my list of tics, I'd started having panic attacks, and developed what I can only describe as acute hearing. My filter for unimportant noise (trees rustling, cars passing, door creaking) vanished, and the world sounded full of attention-requiring detail. My appetite was all but gone. I wasn't trying to lose weight, but after three or four mouthfuls I felt uncomfortably full, and having always been lithe, could now take a child's eye out with my hips. The motions of wellness had deserted me, and I was becoming desensitized to the medicine I'd prescribed. Where previously my drinking had been preceded by an internal debate –

What time is it?
Ah, it's too early.

You think?
Yeah, you should never drink before seven.
Seven?
All right, six.
What about five?
You're on . . . But only if you do some work first . . .

– now it was reduced to –

Should I?
Yeah, why not . . .
(Opens bottle.)

I never wanted to get blotto, I wanted *not* to be in the now, so the aim was to find the right level of drunk and stay there. It would work for a tantalizingly brief window. That one small break when you can be a better you, before you drift into drunk. But once I'd started, the race was on. I was once so drunk I accidentally snorted heroin, and you've got to be moving in several different circles of bad for that to happen.

I'd gone to get some speed from a dealer in Brixton, having got the number from a friend, reasoning that it would help me if I overdid it drink-wise. Unfortunately the dealer was so strung-out he gave me the wrong wrap. Later, having duly overdone it, I chopped it up, briefly noted the colour (it was Demerara sugar, speed was white or, when cut with dextrose, pink), rolled up a tenner and snorted. I knew instantly – uh-oh, this is bad . . .

Pulp Fiction would have you believe snorting smack gives you tasteful nasal stigmata and then, looking pale and pretty, you slump to the ground and your heart stops. In my experience you stagger to the sink, projectile vomit, fall to the floor swearing and drift in and out of consciousness as waves of nausea hit you, and you continue barfing.* Like the syrup of ipecac scene in *Family Guy*. On balance, as salutary lessons go, it was a corker. I don't think I'd have taken smack knowingly – I'd only ever met one smack-head, a theatre tech who got fired for borrowing money from kids in the cast of a panto, and he'd put me right off – but you never know. I can see how if you meet the wrong people at the wrong time, you can get lost. The American writer and ex-junkie Jerry Stahl wrote, 'Heroin makes you feel so good, you feel like calling the phone company and telling them what a good job they're doing.' What self-loathing person wouldn't want that in their day?

I didn't confide in my family for obvious reasons. Me being attacked had been added to the 'we don't talk about it' list, under the pretext of 'not wanting to upset Abi', rather than 'we find this difficult'. There was active disinformation too. A few months after the attack I'd made the trip up North for a family gathering, and a great-uncle said how sorry he was to hear about my 'burglary' and it took me a second to realize, 'Oh right,

---

* I called him the next day and complained. You'd be surprised how few drug dealers have a customer-care department.

that's what he's been told by the family, now what am I meant to do ...?' Of course I toed the party line, and said yes, it was awful, and to my horror was asked follow-up questions – what did they take, what did the police say, have they caught them, with other people joining the circle ... and I had to come up with lie after lie, because I'd committed myself. Sometimes you don't even have to seek a parallel world, it's just handed to you.

By late August, eight months after the attack, the forensic evidence so painstakingly gathered by the SOCOs finally made it to the front of the queue, and someone from the station called (they'd long since stopped coming around – I was no longer a 'hot' case) to inform me that whoever he was, he was 'not known to the police'. Of course, they added casually, he could've just changed cities, or offended elsewhere. She told me that there were political obstacles to the linking of Britain's police forces' databases, and so none of the computers were linked. And the rest was silence.

I got off the phone, and poured myself a drink (that I could do). Such a short call, polite and apologetic – like someone had got lumbered with phoning a patient with bad test results. It never occurred to me to say, 'But you can't give up!' I simply said, 'Thank you for letting me know.'

But case closed. The rest of the world had moved on. And the rest was silence.

There was no getting away from it – having effectively not worked for eight months, I was broke. Granted it was middle-class broke, meaning I was worried about accumulating debt rather than so broke I couldn't afford to drink, but it wasn't looking good . . .

My sister suggested I apply for criminal injuries compensation, but claiming wasn't as easy as it sounded. If I had been an employee it would've been straightforward, but as a self-employed person they wanted tax returns and bank statements going back five years (plus those from the show), multiple forms from doctors ('Your injuries must be verified by the appropriate medical authorities'), crime numbers, copies of my statement and other relevant guff.

If I'd thought the law compartmentalized suffering, I hadn't seen anything yet. The CICB application form included a 'compensation list' tallying how much you'd get for what injury, and their 'multiple injuries formula' – which, despite sounding like they've discovered a way to hurt people en masse, means that you got 100 per cent compensation for the biggest injury, 25 per cent for the second, 15 per cent for the third and nothing after that.

So, say you'd lost an arm and an eye and suffered burns to your torso and had a nervous breakdown you'd get 100 per cent of the highest award – the arm – less for the eye, not much for the burns and zip for the breakdown. A bit like Boots' special offers where the cheapest item is free. With a morbid imagination and their injuries tabulator, you could invent the most bizarre accident combinations and it would cough up an amount – a dog bit you, his owner pushed you out of a window whereupon you punctured a lung and lost your left ear (and remember, players, only the worst three count).

Unfortunately the thought of having to tabulate my own injuries, track down my X-rays and spend days with my accountant drained my will to live. I put it aside for when I was feeling stronger, whenever that was.

I avoided talking to my doctor because I figured he'd tell me to stop drinking, and I had no intention of returning to the Homerton even if my life depended on it. So I did what I'd always done when my back was against the wall. I tried to read my way out of it. I may not have been able to write but I could still read and *someone* must know what to do. Unfortunately pre-Web my choices fell into two distinct categories. The first were academic tomes called things like *Acts of Aggression – Gender Violence in an Urban America* and were stuffed with jargon like 'exogenous latent variables'. One prison study in America had a rapist being asked, 'Why did you rape?' and him answering, 'Because it's fun,' which at least was honest. But not very helpful.

Option two was self-help books that came from shops called things like 'Mysteries' and did at least try to address the world in emotional terms. But the language was that kind of mollifying LA therapy speak circa 1984, designed to tell someone who's been divorced three times that they're learning and growing rather than that they're crap at relationships. There were *Cinderella Complexes, Healing The Shame That Binds You, Why Don't I Feel Better?, Even*

Eagles Need A Push ... all tossing around words like closure, acceptance and healing as if they were genuine wisdoms that had stood the test of time, rather than eighties wish-fulfilments suggesting pain had a full stop, and wellness was something to be achieved. It was a landscape devoid of politics, poetry or art, yet filled to the margin with karma-lite nonsense like 'There's no such thing as coincidence' and 'God never gives you more than you can handle'. Feel the fear and do it anyway. (But what if you're frightened of falling off a tall building?) Do something nice for yourself. (Define nice? I can't even order food.) I probably over-reacted, I've always felt oppressed by bland advice, which starts in childhood with 'Just be yourself' (if I could just be myself we wouldn't be having these problems, now would we?) and 'Just try and enjoy it!', and the ever-popular 'Well, as long as you've done your best...' (define 'best'). Grown-ups, I noticed, tended to give children advice based upon how they *wished* things had been for them, not how it actually was. Otherwise all parents would teach their kids how to punch someone on the nose and run – at least so they'd have a plan B.

The end game came while reading a book (given by a friend) containing affirmations (there's your warning right there) to be said twenty times a day.

For depression sufferers: '*I have the capacity to take in the fullness of life. I lovingly live life to the fullest.*'

For anxiety sufferers: '*I love and approve of myself, and I trust the process of life. I am safe.*'

And for addictions: '*I now discover how wonderful I am. I choose to love and enjoy myself.*'

Now who wouldn't rather head-butt a spike?

Finally, by sheer chance I stumbled across something that broke me open. To ease the monotony of self-help books and academic tomes, I'd been re-reading my top classics and started Dickens' *A Tale of Two Cities*. As a child I'd thought it was about the French Revolution, with a mad lady knitting and a bloody guillotine; now, as an older drunker reader, I realized it was about alcoholic despair . . .

The hero, Sydney Carton, was once a promising young lawyer, but was now an active alcoholic (we don't know why, Dickens favours a standing start) reduced to propping up the career of a much less talented barrister called Mr Skyver, who paid him in beer money. One night, after helping him sort out a big case, Carton staggers home . . .

Waste forces within him, and a desert all around, this man stood still on his way across a silent terrace, and saw for a moment, lying in the wilderness before him, a mirage of honourable ambition, self-denial, and perseverance. In the fair city of this vision, there were airy galleries from which the loves and graces looked upon him, gardens in which the fruits of life hung ripening, waters of Hope that sparkled in his sigh. A moment, and it was gone . . .

I was gripped. That's me! My career was circling the drain too . . .

Climbing to a high chamber in a well of houses, he threw himself down in his clothes on a neglected bed, and its pillow was wet with wasted tears. Sadly, sadly, the sun rose; it rose upon no sadder sight than the man of good abilities and good emotions, incapable of their directed exercise, incapable of his own help and his own happiness, sensible of the blight on him, and resigning himself to let it eat him away.

A century before the 'isms' and psychobabble we take for granted when mapping our interiors, Dickens captured a soul in decline, making despair three-dimensional (*airy galleries*), metaphorical (*Waste forces* and *deserts*) and even tactile (I know that *neglected bed*) and sheer poetry (*waters of Hope that sparkled in his sigh*).

Most acute of all was his grasp of a torment frequently missed by doctors, self-help books and even friends. Often our pain is not the result of not knowing what to do, but of knowing what to do and our inability to do it. Good abilities and good emotions mean nothing if their owner is incapable of their directed exercise. Otherwise we'd all be thin and healthy, and nobody would smoke.

I'd read drunks in books like *Silas Marner*, where they were the bad guy, or in *The Strange Case of Dr Jekyll and Mr Hyde* (a very druggy book), where when he's off his face he's a monster. In a lot of modern American literature drunkenness seemed gay and romantic (Scott Fitzgerald) or bullishly masculine (Hemingway). The *New Yorker*'s coterie of wits, known as the Vicious Circle, including my beloved Dorothy Parker and Robert Benchley, saw drinking, especially during Prohibition, as a way of cocking a snoot at the establishment, and a gateway to wit ('I must get out of these wet clothes into a dry martini' – Benchley), and Edna St Vincent Millay made it sparkle.

> My candle burns at both ends
> It will not last the night;
> But ah, my foes, and oh, my friends –
> It gives a lovely light.

Dickens on the other hand made Carton a sick man, whose drunkenness wasn't due to hedonism or dissolute choices but was something he was in the grip of. I read the passage again and again, and threw myself into Carton's journey. Unfortunately Dickens isn't big on character arcs – nobody really learns or grows, they can only redeem themselves, and for Carton that meant falling in love with a pretty girl and sacrificing himself in a Christlike way:

It is a far, far better thing that I do than I have ever done; it is a far, far better rest that I go to than I have ever known.

I didn't want to die, Christlike or otherwise, but I knew something had to give. Avoiding my friends, I was sinking into social isolation. Mark, concerned at my dropping weight, took me on trips to the supermarket (much appreciated), and there was the odd hot supper and lots of booze, but conversation was ring-fenced; stay away from the past, or as he put it: 'You're not going to go round dragging *that* up again, are you?'

More in desperation than hope, I returned to my GP and asked for help. He shamefacedly admitted there was no one place he could refer me to – no integrated treatments for trauma sufferers. The best he could do was treat each symptom in turn. If I wanted a talking cure, that meant seeing a clinical psychologist and an eight-month waiting list. The best fast thing on offer was a six-week course for people with phobias. I said yes (I was phobic about being attacked, after all).

It turned out to be an early variant of Cognitive Behavioural Therapy (CBT). I traipsed up the Holloway Road, to the Royal Free Hospital, but it looked closed. I entered tentatively and was told by the bored-looking security guard that it was shut, but there were people on the fourth floor. I made my way up, and along a series of echoey grey lino corridors, an NHS version of *The Shining*, until I found Blu-tacked handwritten signs directing me towards the door of Dr Harris.

I knocked and a young blonde woman welcomed me with a profusion of apologies – this was the only space she could get, everyone else had moved– she was between placements. We began and I 'fessed up about the drinking, and to my relief she said I was unhappy rather than weak or bad (excessive drinking always comes with a sense of shame) and she gave me some diversionary tactics for the hand flapping – tapping my head. By the end of the session I realized she'd also taught me the single most important criterion when choosing someone to tell all your deeply hidden inside stuff to – are they happier than you? If they're not, get out of there fast. But if they're contented, cheerful and act with good conscience then stick around.

At my last session but one, I asked if I could keep on seeing her – the tapping was helping and I said I'd pay if necessary. She said no. She liked working on the NHS and if she cheated and let me stay on for another couple of sessions, someone who was as upset as I was when I arrived would have to wait (see – conscience). She arranged for me go to a posher psychiatric place with a view to getting some long-term private therapy.

Two weeks later, at the posher psychiatric place in Swiss Cottage, I was led into a room and pointed to a seat in the middle. A short white man wearing a pin-striped suit was sitting to one side. 'Do you mind us filming your assessment?' he asked. 'For training purposes only.' I looked up and saw a video camera pointing at me, its red light blinking. 'Of course I do!' What survivor of sexual assault would want to be filmed? He turned off the camera and said nothing. Then he said more nothing. Then he added to the nothing with more nothing.

'Is this how it works?' I asked. 'You just look at me and say nothing?'

He scribbled in a notepad and said nothing. Eventually I cracked. 'How helpful do you think you saying nothing and staring at me with your rat-like eyes actually is?' He scribbled more notes.

It wasn't my finest hour, but when I told my counsellor during my final session she laughed.

'Did you really say "rat-like eyes"?'

'Well, they were rat-like,' I grumbled.

She told me it was probably a deliberate strategy – do nothing to see what the patient brings into the room. It's meant to be very revealing. (Yes, just what trauma patients need – to be put under stress, so someone can 'gauge their reactions'.) The bigger posher psychiatric place wrote to me a week later and recommended I came along five times a week for three years, and enclosed details of charitable grants that might help with costs. Well, I was crazy, but I wasn't that crazy.

Still, the counselling had given me a new lease of semi-life. I started believing that if I could just get my drinking back to pre-war limits, there might be a way out.

Then a stroke of luck. Some work writing ads for a comedian in the US dropped into my lap. It was light-hearted, well paid and I'd be writing with a friend, so there was no locking myself away and getting drunk. There was turning up hung-over, however. Sitting there, sweaty and muddle-headed in a morning writing session, my friend made the most radical suggestion I'd ever heard. Why don't you stop drinking?

What?

I said I didn't want to stop, I just wanted it to be like it used to be. He reiterated the suggestion. How bad could it be? Now the extremism of it appealed to me, but I wasn't convinced – controlling my drinking seemed the way to go. Stopping was, well, frightening.

A week later I caught sight of myself in a full-length mirror, propped against a wall in the front room. Usually when we look in a mirror it's intentional – we're putting on make-up, checking our hair, smartening our clothes. It's why when we catch unexpected glances of ourselves in a shop window we get such a jolt – 'Dear God, is that really me?'

I was wearing jogging bottoms, a tattered and stained Winnie the Pooh T-shirt and eating baked beans *out of the can* because I couldn't be arsed to heat them up.

> . . . sensible of the blight on him, and resigning himself to let it eat *him away* . . .

So on the 20th of December I did what Sidney Carton couldn't. I stopped drinking. Cold.

Chapter Nine

No one lies so boldly as an indignant man

FRIEDRICH NIETZSCHE

DRINKERS DRINK FOR every occasion. You drink because you're happy, sad, angry, overworked, under-worked, stressed, bored, etc. . . . there is nothing (except driving) that doesn't go better with booze. Your drinking pals will always top up your glass. Drink's not like food – no one ever says, 'Go on, have another chicken.'

> You drink because you're happy
> You drink because you're sad
> You drink because you're lonely
> You drink because you're mad
> You drink because you want to
> You drink because you must
> You drink because it's easy
> You drink because you're bust.

Cheap doggerel, and even I wasn't happy with the last line, but I needed something to repeat when I wanted a drink, because when you first stop drinking, you're constantly not drinking. You're not drinking on a Friday night, or a Sunday afternoon. You're not necking one when you're pissed off, or because you're listening to music. You're not meeting friends in pubs, or stumbling around the flat in the afternoon. You're not just nipping into the off-licence, or pouring a glass because it's seven.

Sober is a new constant, and its novelty is a wonder. Psychologically, the simple act of not pouring gallons of depressants into the system lifts the spirits. Physically the body bounces back like it's been leaning into a headwind. I looked better, my eyes were clearer, my skin springier, even my posture improved. Substituting food for drink meant my weight started to creep up, my breasts returned and my buttocks swelled pleasingly.

I went from constantly not having enough money to having more than I expected. I stopped worrying that I had enough in, or manipulating people into coming to a really horrid pub because it was last orders, or leaving the party so I could go home and get as drunk as I really wanted.

I forgot about being attacked and being broke. Stopping drinking is nothing short of liberation. Poor Carton.

The downside is you can't sleep. 'No one ever died from insomnia,' sober people tell you, and although you want to punch them because you're tired, you believe them because they're happier and healthier than you. Drunk sleep is more or less a blackout and I have no recollection of dreams after the attack – I woke up disturbed and sweaty a few times but with no memory as to why.

But once I slept I dreamt, which was a double-edged sword. Sometimes it was beautifully vivid, like *The Wizard of Oz* when it switches to Technicolor, but other times it was plain disturbing. I've never had a full-blown TV nightmare, where, apparently, you flash back to handheld shots of a terrifying incident (from a distorted angle), wake at the critical moment, sit upright and scream. My dreams would start off normally – I'd be in a park, or on a bus. Then, with the illogical ebb and flow of the imagination, I'd be in another time – my voice wouldn't work, or I'd realize I wasn't in England but in a far-off land with no money, no language and no way of getting home. Characters like ticket inspectors or waiters who seemed helpful would change into sinister figures, mouths distorting, eyes bulging. I had a series of dreams where I was followed by an amorphous blob. Not a shadow, they're flat. But something dark and oily that slipped out of sight when you tried to glimpse it. Several times I found myself in a dilapidated room with an uneven floor and plasterboard and I'd think I was alone, only to discover a wordless stranger seated in a corner, watching me.

Despite feeling jet-lagged during the day, nothing made me want to start drinking. This was too exciting, too enervating and too inclusive. I began making friends who didn't drink, and learnt new ways of socializing – coffee and cake not booze and kebabs.

I reflected on my past and made a list of all the times I'd nearly died and next to it a list of all the men I'd slept with if only out of politeness. (The second list was shorter than the first, but at least as frightening.) The previous goal of using drink to collapse the day in on itself was in sharp reverse. Now the days were long, and the evenings even longer. I lost my ability to watch crap TV, but learned how to meditate. I started reading, started remembering, started enjoying. It was much easier than I'd thought precisely because it was so extreme. There's no guesswork in 'no'. No internal debate, no promises or strategies to be devised. It's just no thank you. Why doesn't everyone do this? I thought. Drinking is for mugs. Marx said religion was the opium of the masses. Well, I think you'll find it's beer.

I began to have 'real' conversations with people who were honest about who they were, what had happened and why they wanted to change. When someone's told you that they went to see their mother dying of cancer in hospital just so they could steal her morphine, polite conversation seems subsequently pointless.

Soon I bubbled with vivacious 'knowingness', bringing all the unpleasant traits of the recently converted. First, I began to notice how much everybody else drank. In a generalized way I noticed how many pubs there were, and I'd image the high street if every one was, say, a stationers, or a hardware store. There was a cartoon in the *Daily Mirror*** where a man asks direction from a vicar and Andy Capp.† The vicar says, 'Turn left at St Mark's, cross the road to St Angeline's and it's by St Peter's.' Capp says, 'Turn left at the Red Lion, cross at the King's Head and it's next to the Dog and Duck.' I had a similar internal map, with the added details of who did lock-ins, which kebab houses sold beer from under the counter and where you could get carry-outs after 11.00 p.m.

In more unpleasantly particular ways I noticed how much my family drank. I knew we drank – it wasn't a secret. Not since Mum died had there been a family occasion that didn't involve getting drunk. Not 'a drink' – getting drunk.

'How come Abi doesn't drink but you all do?' asked a woman at a barbecue.

'Because we're all alcoholics,' said Mark, 'ha ha ha.'

People who drink become trapped in a particularly distorted reality. When you're 'up' you can't remember what it's like to be down, and when you're down, vice versa. A drunk will pour out their troubles to you one day, telling you you're their best friend, their only friend, and the next day when you follow up, brush off your concerns, telling you they're fine fine fine, making you feel silly for asking. More often than not, evenings would end with my sister saying, 'We didn't turn out too badly – none of us are

---

* Which Dad got – the *Guardian* was Mum's.
† 'Oh, Andy Capp . . . you wife-beating drunk' – Homer Simpson.

murderers or thieves,' and me trying not to say, 'I'm all for setting the bar low, but come on.' It was never less than sad. But it was also boring, and although objectionably sober and upbeat, I had problems of my own.

After a year, my original sober high wore off, and I wanted to deal with why I drank – and it wasn't all to do with being attacked. First up: boundaries. It had never occurred to me I was entitled to them. My talent was to keep out of sight. Dad's drinking had been controlled by Mum, but since she'd died, despite health warnings from doctors, a stroke, consistent driving drunk, nothing dulled his passion for drinking. The independence not drinking gave me seemed to antagonize him, and his behaviour toward me became increasingly erratic.

So when one afternoon he called to 'cheer me up' with a joke about oral sex, the inner dialogue I'd absorbed since childhood ('Forget about it . . . ignore him . . . it's only Dad') didn't work and I allowed myself to consider that, hmmmm, even if I hadn't been attacked, fathers shouldn't phone their daughters to tell them jokes about cocksucking.

I called some women friends. Is this OK? Does your father talk to you like this? To a woman they said dear God no, their fathers wouldn't dream of it. The other shoe, as our American cousins would put it, was dropping. There was a long lead in. Earlier that summer, he'd phoned me on a sunny day – not to find out how I was, but to tell me what a 'great nipple count there was out there' and chuckle at my discomfiture.

Later at a family meal (sans Dad) I told Mark and Harriet how disturbing I found this, and asked for their support. 'It's only Dad,' came the familiar refrain, 'ignore him.'

Then my brother's wife, who barely spoke, suddenly chipped in. 'It's not right,' she said. 'You do know that?'

Someone from outside the family who'd met Dad had validated my feelings! It was transformative particularly because she didn't like me very much. Yet even she didn't take it seriously. When I asked later, 'Do you change the way you dress when you're around him?' she said, 'Yes, but it doesn't bother me,' and I replied, 'How do you think it feels if you're his daughter?' she just shrugged.

As I was leaving, my sister took me aside and gave me her advice – get a boyfriend. He 'stopped all that' with her once she got married. Right, so to be free of my father I had to belong to another man. Nice one.

Following that debacle there seemed little point in going to either of them for moral support, re. the cock-sucking joke. So I wrote a short – not angry – fifteen-line letter, asking him to stop talking to me like this, and adding I thought his years of reading nothing but hard-core pornography had blunted his sense of what was appropriate. He needed to talk to somebody.

I was trembling when I wrote it and knew I was crossing the Rubicon. I heard nothing. Then a few days later, when I was opening my mail over a cup of tea, there was his reply.

Three pages of single-spaced attack,* calling me a liar a cheat, a fantasist, and threatening me with legal action. He said he thought people in my business understood 'risqué and blue' language, and claimed he'd only started reading pornography after my mother died, what did I expect him to do then – visit prostitutes?

I was staggered. Not the abuse, that was familiar, but the lies. I'm a good liar, he taught me that – you stick as close to the truth as possible. He was seriously claiming he'd only started reading it after Mum died? This was insane. I knew aged twelve we were going on holiday to Denmark so he could buy even harder-core stuff.

He said it was an outrageous claim, no one had ever told him this before . . .

I stopped again.

Really?

Only the week before he'd introduced a new house guest to me and Mark, while we were over for supper. She was seventeen, Hungarian and pretty. She'd turned up with a scrap of paper with the names of previous occupants, who had probably lived there in the sixties. He let her in and gave her a room. Telling us he laughed, saying he thought it was his birthday because he got a massive erection (in case we were any doubt, he acted out the 'big erection').

Mark phoned the next day to say it wasn't appropriate.

Dad ended his screed by saying I was greedy, thankless,

* Incidentally, all in past simple.

yadda yadda yadda, and I'd clarified some things in his mind and he'd be speaking to his lawyer in the morning, i.e., that was me out of the will, and away from my mother's things. I knew he was saying that to hurt me, but apart from her Folio Society books (especially her complete Samuel Pepys diaries) there was nothing I wanted. The trouble with free money is it costs too much.

When I called Mark I was still jittery, but to my amazement he already knew. Dad, bizarrely (or not, for my family), had sent him and Harriet carbon copies of his letter. Mark kept saying, 'But I told him last week.'

When I got off the phone I had a moment of calm. 'This means I never have to see him again.' Any other time of my life I'd have poured a drink, but I went and fed the ducks in the park instead. Tossing the crusts in, I was all the time monitoring: Nope, I feel fine . . . Ah, yes, still feel fine . . . This is great . . . (Don't forget the small one at the back) . . . Still feel fine . . . What a lovely day . . .

I'd done my grieving years ago. As a teenager on the top deck of the 88 bus coming home from school one day I worked it out: on balance, I might love my father, but I didn't like him. Now I didn't love him either. Free at last, free at last, thank God Almighty . . .

Harriet wrote back to him commending me for sticking my head above the parapet and saying she couldn't believe her eyes – 'Are you threatening my little sister?' For a brief flicker, I had hopes something might happen. But it was a false alarm. They carried on seeing him (and if possible drank more) and it was brushed under the carpet, to be passed off to wider circles as a petty dispute.

I didn't care, I was free and still revelling in my new-found orphandom when news arrived from a friend of my mother's. Barely a week after my letter, and in complete ignorance of what had happened with me, she'd visited Dad and met the Hungarian girl, who, she noticed, couldn't speak English. She watched my father pretending to be a kindly gentleman, while making remarks of an explicitly sexual nature in front of the poor girl (the fact that she couldn't understand what he was saying added to his fun). Disturbed, she wrote him a gentle letter, expressing concern, and offering details of a friend who could speak Hungarian. He responded with a typical attack, telling her she was lying, instructing her to butt out and mind her own business. I let out a sigh. My mother's friend was a Quaker – and not a Nixon Quaker, a proper Paul Eddington type, not given to starting trouble. It really, *really* wasn't me.

Six more months of not drinking and not seeing my father saw the stirrings of life and even sexual feeling. I was working, earning money and felt new green shoots of optimism. Maybe the worst was over.

Then the police called out of the blue and said they wanted to speak to me.

'Have you got him?' I asked. 'No,' they said, but wanted to drop by. The following Thursday, two officers from Stoke Newington police station turned up. I apologized for not having a sofa, and made them tea and they sat on my bed (still in the front room), and told me they were going to do a *Crimewatch* segment on the Finsbury Park rapist (as they called him). They apologized again for bringing up a 'painful subject' and admitted they still weren't sure my attack was related to the other two that weekend but wanted to go through my statement, and see if I'd remembered anything new in the meantime.

We chatted for an hour or so, and as usual, the worst questions were the 'What did he taste like?' and 'What did he smell like?', more affecting than Proustian tea and cake. I passed on the chance to give a silhouetted TV interview and as they left they apologized again.

'I'm fine,' I reassured them.

'You look it,' they said. They'd tracked down the other two victims. One had been a student at St Martins School of Art (very prestigious place) but following the rape dropped out of college, had a nervous breakdown and was holed up in a bed-sit in Brighton, on benefit. The other had given up her career in London and was also living on benefit, staying at her parents'. Both were too scared to go out alone. It didn't make me feel better. It made me feel angry.

I avoided the broadcast, I wasn't up to seeing the crime reconstructions, so I don't know if my case was mentioned. I received no feedback from the police, so assumed the trail had gone cold again.

Then as life began settling down to a post-dad, post-*Crimewatch* normality, I broke the writer's eleventh commandment.

Chapter Ten

Thou shalt not sleep with anyone who has
more problems than yourself.

TRADITIONAL

NEVER GO OUT with a next-door neighbour, that's my advice. You don't need to have been attacked or recovering from a drink problem – never go out with the boy next door. And if he's a comedian, and you're thinking about going out with him, burn everything you own and move now, it'll be cheaper. Because when it goes wrong, somebody's going to need a new address. It started with ecstasy or MDMA and ended with weed (so, no warning signs for me to miss there).

He was a comedian and we got on really well as mates – it was great having someone around who was in the same business, had a good sense of humour (by which I mean he laughed at my jokes) and came with a film collection, which coupled with mine meant we had a library. I didn't date performers as a rule, because experience told me that in any relationship someone's got to be decent, kind, honest and sensitive and chances are it wasn't going to be me. Plus, having been out with performers in the past, I'd found they were incredibly self-absorbed, neurotic and obsessed with their careers, instead of being incredibly self-absorbed, neurotic and obsessed with my career. And just as drugs of a feather have to stick together – pot-heads can't date coke-heads – so writers and comedians don't mix.

Then came E. I'd been drink- and drug-free for a while. Clean and sober had become the new norm, or in other words, the novelty had worn off. I'd never believed LSD was in the same category as smack or crack or even drink, and from what I'd read, Ecstasy was in the same ball park. So I said yes when he suggested popping a pill. Or two. Or three. Or four. In the end I'm not sure, but we tripped sixteen hours and it remains as profound an emotional and physical experience as I've had.

Ecstasy defies simile, it provokes the *opposite* of anxiety – not the egocentricity of cocaine, but an expansive sense of well-being. After my third pill I would've called the phone company to tell them what a great job they were doing, but was certain they knew I loved them without me having to. We took E many times after that, trying to recapture the first fine careless rapture but it was never the same.

I've since discovered the US Food and Drug Administration has approved MDMA (the active ingredient in Ecstasy) for treating post-traumatic stress in soldiers and survivors of sexual assault. (And under the Bush administration, no less.)*

'Drugs can be controlled but that doesn't stop them being useful,' said Dr John Halpern, a psychiatrist at the University of Harvard's McLean Hospital. Another American doctor, Julie Holland of New York University, wrote: 'Walls form around trauma – like a scar – MDMA helps people feel calm and comfortable enough to explore painful things that are hard to talk about.' My experience exactly. But however therapeutic I found taking E, it is not the basis for a relationship.

Simon and I were together for eight happy months and twenty-two miserable ones. Having completely missed out on the dating stage, going straight for romantic love (drug-induced romantic love), we barely knew each other. His childhood was as damaging and extreme as mine, and as time went on, our behaviour consistently manifested itself in stark contradiction to the idea that we were 'made for each other'. He cheated on me. I cheated on him, and we hurt each other hugely. Once the high was gone the sex was awful, and we went from being inseparable to not talking to smoking lots of weed and finally buying an Xbox so we could be in each other's company without having to be in each other's presence. My awkwardness returned along with my trauma – I lost weight, couldn't sleep, started having flashbacks, and worst of all, dissociative episodes became more and more frequent.

* 'Treating agony with ecstasy', David Adam, *Guardian*, 17 February 2005.

Living next door meant avoiding each other was impossible, and the falling-apart dance (breaking up, getting back together, promises being made, it's all right now, breaking up, getting back together, promises being made, it's all right now) was excruciating. As with all relationships, you're not giving up what it is, you're giving up what you'd hoped it would be, and I thought it proved I was cured, and capable of loving and being loved.

I was heartbroken, and what little facility I had for work vanished. I was dropped by my agent. The familiar slide into money problems and depression began, this time accompanied by an anguished cry of 'Not again!' With a late epiphany I realized I was trying to get my past needs met in the present and as the facade of wellness crumbled I knew that was it. I sank lower and lower until one night I heard him through the wall having sex with an ex-girlfriend and completely broke down. The flat had lost any semblance of refuge and had become the place where bad things had happened. I dreaded coming home, and dreaded waking up. One of us had to move, and as I was the one renting I packed my trunk and said goodbye to the circus despite having no money, no home and nowhere to go.

I had only two things going for me, I still wasn't drinking, and I had friends.

Chapter Eleven

**Sometimes it is hard to distinguish between
a respiration from God, and a suggestion
from the Devil.**

JOHN DONNE *PREACHED AT THE SPITAL,
22 APRIL 1622*

ONE OF THE extraordinary constancies in middle-class
people's lives is the niceness of their surroundings. They
grow up with nice furniture, eat nice meals, go to nice
restaurants. When they order things people are nice on
the phone – and should you choose to go to therapy, you
may find pot plants, reading material and of course nice
furniture in the waiting room. Everything in your physical
surrounding reinforces the sense that you are a person of
worth – and it does this without you noticing. For those
without, however, the experience is the opposite, especially
when it comes to mental health. I asked a doctor at the
Waterlow hospital's mental-health unit why the walls were
painted such a sickly puce, cream and grey green –
somewhere between an artificial limb and a battleship –
and he told me it was important not to have colours that
'stimulated' people and that these were calming, which

I'm sure is true – most clinically depressed people give the appearance of calm by neither talking nor moving.

It's the same with the DSS. The offices might now have ticker boards and electronic 'next number called' signs, but the dreariness is immortal. I hadn't claimed benefit for years. I'd been laid off several times when I first left school during what is now euphemistically called the 'great labour-market shakeout' of the 1980s, and was in and out of the DHSS (as it was then) like a pinball. With three million unemployed the offices were busy, and claiming was straightforward. Everyone was in the same boat and gallows humour abounded. For example:

Q: What's green and doesn't go far?
A: A giro.
Q: What's green and gets you pissed?
A: A giro.
Q: What's black and white and shuffles?
A: A dole queue.

'A bloke jumps into the Mersey, screaming, "I can't take it any more, they're working me to death." A bystander jumps in. "Don't try and save me," cries the drowning man. "I'm not," says the other, "I just want to know where you work . . ."'

And so on. Now the humour was gone. Yesteryear's potpourri of accents had blossomed into a Tower of Babel and the locals, black and white, simmered with resentment. Outside people still smoked roll-ups and drank the occasional beer. Inside, people went from queue to queue, amid the murmuring and chitchat that accompanies endless waiting around. Depressingly there were more kids running around with sticky faces and clothes dusted in crisp crumbs, loudly playing hide and seek behind the fixed furniture, or else sitting quietly drawing pictures on A4 office paper in blue DSS half-biro.

To discourage new claimants, rafts of new regulatory hoops had been put in place, reflecting the entitlement 'determinants' of successive governments as they sought to cut welfare without actually means-testing. In practice it means the more that was wrong with your life, the more hoops you had to jump through to prove it. Previously I'd been unemployed, now I was a Job Seeker (just as refugees were now Asylum-seekers – there was a lot of seeking going on) entitled to £45.00 Job Seeker's Allowance a week. I was advised I *might* be entitled to incapacity benefit, but how much and what type would need working out.

I was sent to another desk and told what forms to request, and while waiting for my number to be called, a fellow-traveller and seasoned veteran warned me. 'Everyone gets turned down for everything first time round,' he said, 'so they can test whether you're *really* serious.'

I got the forms and filled them in. Whereas in the rest of life you try to be positive and act with hope in your heart, in DSS land, that'll cost you. You have to be the most miserable broken-down socially useless and incompetent being you can possibly be, and draw attention to every panic attack, nightmare, deep dark thought you've ever had. If you weren't crazy to begin with, hey, if you become morbidly depressed – you could get an extra £11.60 care allowance.

One of the blowbacks of the benefit system is that making it harder to get it *doesn't* make fewer people want it, it makes those who've managed to get it loath to give it up.

But I was a long way away from benefit stagnation. I was still sliding downhill, with no meaningful friction to slow me down. Living on sofa beds and floors and being abjectly poor – and I mean proper working-class poor rather than I-can-only-afford-one-holiday-a-year poor – was a disturbing new place. I borrowed a little money here and there, but the peculiar thing when you're skint and you know rich people is that they're the ones you avoid. Someone who's about on the same level, or just above, you feel fine borrowing two hundred pounds from, borrowing from a millionaire makes you feel pathetic.

I began selling off my possessions. The earrings and clothes didn't bother me, neither did the stuffed fish I'd been given as a christening present,* but letting go of my vinyl was a wrench ... but I needed the money. The difference between getting by and not getting by can be as little as £17.63. (I know because that's the exact amount

---

* My godfather had bought a job lot at auction and gave me a trout caught in 1912. Got £180 at auction.

of a bill I couldn't pay that reduced me to tears.) You quietly exclude yourself from 'normal' culture because you can't afford it. Not only do you not go to the cinema, when you pass it you don't think, 'What's on?' You don't look in shop windows, and unless you watch TV on a Saturday evening with adverts for chicken and cereals (and maybe the odd soap powder) every advert serves as a taunt. I ended up playing a game I hadn't played since my early twenties – watching Channel 4 and seeing how many ads were for things I could afford. ('Car . . . no. Oh, another car . . . no . . . Waitrose . . . no . . .') Living on the fortnight as they call it.

It's usually around now that someone says 'that which does not destroy you makes you stronger', and I have to resist saying, 'Spoken like a German.' It doesn't make you stronger, it makes you limping and mean. Nothing about scraping by is good for the soul – it doesn't encourage you to play, dream or vaguely hope, and you pull on failure like damp clothes every bloody morning. I even took a cleaning job for cash in hand. Given that's what I did when I left school the sense of failure was complete. From here to the West End and back again. I think this is where we came in.

I got by because of friends (the comfortable but not too wealthy ones), who plied me with food, company and nights out. One close female friend let me stay for over a month despite living in the tiniest flat in North London, where even the mice had to crouch, and I was an inconvenience, but was never made to feel less than welcome. Plus she let me ramble on unreasonably the way you do after a relationship.

Mentally, though, it was beginning to get sticky. Not having my own roof and front door was exacerbating my distress. I told my GP I was having thoughts darker than I was comfortable with.

'How dark?'

'I want it all to stop.'

'Define stop?'

'If I didn't wake up I wouldn't be sorry.'

He referred me to the Waterlow hospital's mental-health unit as a suicide risk. It wasn't an ambulance job – I got the bus, and on arrival handed my letter to the receptionist who told me it would be a minimum four-hours wait. 'So, this is for the suicidal . . . but patient.' I smiled, and if she'd had a notepad she'd have scribbled in it.

It was a fairly horrid wait to be honest, there was nothing to read, not even a *Woman's Weekly* to beat yourself over the head with. I knew I wasn't ready for the off. I'd not counted pills out or cut myself, I just wasn't in control of my mind's recesses. Oddly for someone who has to see films to the end, the thought of checking out before my own end didn't strike me as irrational.

Eventually two stressed-out young doctors were found, who referred me upstairs to a clinical psychologist. Older, with a longer title and bigger office, he said I wasn't suicidal, but had some variant of PTSD and prescribed me sertraline (an SSRI, part of the Prozac family) and suggested I call a new women's therapy centre that ran groups for survivors of sexual assault. He deduced lack of housing was making things worse and wrote me a very supportive letter – 'to whom it may concern'.

I didn't like the sertraline, it had all the disorientating qualities of a street drug, but none of the high. But I caught a break when friends announced they were going to Australia, and asked whether I'd like to house-sit for three months. An address to myself for three whole months? Now I had a phone, a front door and space to think.

I decided to take stock. I was sober and adding up my allowance and cash in hand gave me sixty-five pounds a week, which because my mother had brought me up not to lose the Second World War was just enough. Hungry? Two carrots, an onion, some orange lentils and a stock cube. Boil, blend, dollop of yoghurt and slice of bread – cheap as. Mince, potatoes, ox tail, and if you don't get eight meals out of a chicken you're not really trying.

Where to live was the issue. When people think of social housing they think of the council, and maybe housing associations. But it's an infinitely more complex world than that, reflecting the repertoire of different needs in a modern city. You've got your bed and breakfasts if you're desperate and malleable. There are halfway houses for people coming out of prison, or with drug problems, or rough sleepers. There's women's refuges, and charities favouring the elderly, sheltered accommodation, shared housing, semi-independent living and long-running phil-anthropic organizations like the Peabody Estates.*

'Oh, you'll never get in there,' laughed my sister-in-law, reminding me why we didn't get on.

I spent days wading through forms, and applying where I was eligible. 'As long as it isn't a bail hostel,' I thought, 'I'll be OK.' As tasks go it would have been a lot more depressing had not all the people I spoke to been sympathetic and helpful, passing me new numbers, suggesting places to call. Several told me that had I applied directly after being attacked I'd have been re-housed immediately, and all reassured me I had a good case. Unlike people who work for the DSS those in charities are allowed to express their feelings. A former employee of the DSS told me they're trained not to emote. Even if the person is suicidal and desperate for news about their claim, and they have information in front of them, they can't even hint.

I found the mere action of doing something made me feel better. Then I started group therapy.

---

* Established by the London-based American banker George Peabody in 1862. As of 2005 it managed over nineteen thousand properties in London housing nearly fifty thousand people. Now that's how to spend a bonus.

Chapter Twelve

Don't say the old lady screamed.
Bring her on and let her scream.

MARK TWAIN

THE THERAPY WAS for women survivors of sexual assault, and I began with a sense of trepidation, which I'm sure was shared by the rest of our tiny damaged circle. On my first day I did a head count, it was me and four traumatized women (which makes five traumatized women). The room was small and Formica'd with dry air that cracked your lips because the windows didn't open for security reasons, and a dead pot plant. Our therapist wore opaque tights and spoke in that softy voice and tilty-head way that's meant to make you seem empathetic, but makes you look like a spaniel. I wasn't sure if she was happier than me, or what her role was, or what the dynamic was meant to be, but I was willing to give it a go. I harboured hopes that it would be healing to be around people who'd get 'it', that shared experience would create a sense of belonging, but to expect individuals with nothing in common save the worst thing that's ever happened to them to find a natural accord is at best naive. I imagine one reason there are so few effective pressure groups for the survivors of sexual assault is the catchment group is too disparate, and the fallout too catastrophic. We sat in a circle for an hour every Thursday (we weren't allowed to speak to each other outside of the room) but rather than tea and empathy the sessions were often scratchy in a passive-aggressive huffing and puffing sort of way.

I didn't have much in common with the Spanish mother of three who'd been raped by her husband but thought the children should carry on seeing him because 'they need a father'. Or the upper-class woman who'd been raped by her coke-dealing boyfriend, loathed poor people and arrived in a Chelsea tractor. The youngest woman was in her early twenties and had been raped by the friend of a friend, after a party. Like me, she'd hit the bottle and was drinking furiously, chastising herself constantly ('stupid stupid stupid') and worrying about the time she was taking off work – what would they do without her? I did my best to tell her how much I'd drunk, and how much better I'd felt since I stopped, but it was too soon for her to hear and she carried on torturing herself like a bird in a net.

I'm not sure I contributed much, except listening. Their pain seemed raw and physical, mine seemed psychological and I couldn't get over a slight sense of being 'other'. I'd been sexually assaulted but not actually raped so didn't share the physical pain of invasion, or the worries about pregnancy and disease. Plus, I was the only one who didn't know my attacker so I wasn't being torn apart by guilt. The quietest woman was Ethiopian, and who had been attacked not in Africa, but here. An Ethiopian man had talked to her at a community gathering and then days later popped around to her house, talked his way in and attacked her. She didn't say anything because he was a prominent member of the community and she was alone, and in contrast to the younger woman's dizzying energy projected a tired despair and was so softly spoken you could barely hear her.

She was an unlikely saviour. When talking about why she fled to the UK, I said, 'Mengistu?'* and her eyes lit up. I'd heard of him? I said, 'Yes, yes,' and her confidence picked up, and she started talking about the famine, and how she got out, and we all listened. Outside, breaking all the rules, we stopped for a chat and I was bemoaning my homelessness.

'Have you tried MIND?' she said, pointing across the road. 'They helped me.'

MIND is a charity that, according to its mission statement, 'campaigns on behalf of those with mental illness'. Its Islington offices were in a shambolic Edwardian house

---

* The ruthless dictator of Ethiopia during time of the 1984 'Band Aid' famine (having fled the country, he now lives in Zimbabwe as a guest of Robert Mugabe).

with threadbare carpet not unlike the one I grew up in. What would've been the dining room was the reception area and the bedrooms were offices and in the basement there was a healthy (i.e., non-fry-up) cafe. With a general-health clinic two doors down and the therapy centre opposite, this stretch of street represented the quiet face of social services.

I wasn't sure this was the place for me – I was actually worried that I wasn't mad enough.* But from this moment on, my life changed for the better. Unlike the social services, whose main goal seems to be to get you to go to somebody else ('not our department'), the MIND staff, bearing those job descriptions you see in the *Guardian* on a Thursday, were empathetic, non-patronizing and gratifyingly practical.

It became clear after a quick chat that I needed to re-brand my suffering. I'd been thinking of myself as a victim of sexual assault – I should have been playing the crazy card. Without my asking they said they'd help me with my housing *and* benefit, and made an appointment for me to come back with my official paperwork.

Really? You'll help? I'd been so used to doing every-thing on my own, learning as I went along, that this blew me away. It was like wandering into a magical new kingdom, where hope thrived and falafel was served.

On my return, they painstakingly showed me the bureaucratic ropes (ropes I've passed on to others in my

* Don't even think it.

time), explaining how the benefit system is meant to work, and how it actually works. Expanding on the 'everyone gets turned down first time' they taught me that when applying for anything (housing, incapacity benefit) you photocopy your forms before you send them in, so when you get turned down and have to appeal, you can repeat yourself exactly. (It was a dance that went on for nine months before I was finally moved from JSA to incapacity benefit – 'on the sick'.)

All the staff at MIND were irrepressibly helpful. That's not to say there weren't politics. Charities have their share of squabbling, but as an organization, and as individuals, MIND was committed to helping, and protecting the unloved. Sara, the centre's boss, had previously worked for the council, so as gamekeeper turned poacher was ideally suited to rattle some cages. She phoned the housing department on my behalf.

'This is as clear a case of need as I have ever seen,' she said. 'She was attacked by a rapist in her own home, man.'

Armed with supporting letters from doctors and psychologists, Sara and MIND delivered the barely imaginable in months. A one-bedroomed flat in a large council estate.

While I was house-sitting I was told Dad had been admitted to hospital, having collapsed on Christmas Day and found on the floor, both legs swollen up. Neighbours called an ambulance. When it arrived the ambulance staff helped him into a chair, but he refused to move.

'I'm not going to hospital unless my GP says so.'

'What?' said the ambulance staff.

'I'm not going, unless my GP says so.'

The ambulance team, slightly stunned, waited while the doctor was called, but after twenty minutes said, 'This is ridiculous,' and left. Half an hour later, the locum doctor arrived fresh from the dinner table, practically wearing his Christmas paper hat, and took one look at him. 'You should be in hospital,' and walked out in disgust.

'All right, I'll go, then,' said Dad, and another ambulance was called.

He was taken to intensive care, and having passed on a message that he 'was not minded to see me' ('Well, I wouldn't want to get stuck in that long queue of visitors,' I cackled rather meanly) settled in, clicking his fingers at the nurses. None of this affected me until Harriet showed up. She'd given up her holiday with her husband to look after him. I wasn't surprised. Neither was I surprised that he wouldn't let her use his car to get to the hospital, forcing her to take two buses there and back every day.

'I warn you,' she said when she came round to see me, 'I'm dealing with this by getting drunk.' She wasn't exaggerating, and our drunk bar is higher than most.

Then Mark sent me a letter calling me a 'loser and a user' because while he'd been on holiday, I'd borrowed a book without asking. Before I had time to react, two friends, a writer and an actress, died. They were both talented, bright, funny, kind, horribly damaged people. Dan had fallen drunkenly downstairs and broken his neck, Charlotte was found dead in her flat. Clarification if clarification was needed that not everybody makes it to the other side. I made a decision. When I moved I was going to keep my address a secret. I felt guilty about my sister, but just couldn't bear it any more. It took me days to make the decision, but the effect was astonishing. It was liberation. No, it was like running into sunshine . . .

I used to joke that my mother, being liberal, sent me to a comprehensive so that I could be beaten up by children of all different backgrounds. But as it turned out, black kids didn't seem to notice class, and the ones who went for me were poor and white – free school meals and homemade tattoos whose fathers were active in the NF and BNP. ('My dad hates to see a white man sweeping the streets,' said Lee, a plump white girl. 'That's a black man's job.')

I'd been to a lot of council estates in my time. Friends from school lived on estates, and in the eighties I did pirate radio from a concrete hellhole called the North Peckham Estate (where Damilola Taylor was murdered). Jeremy Hardy once said that instead of nuclear bombs that kill people and leave buildings standing, the world needed a bomb that left people standing and killed architects. North Peckham Estate was just such a place, a bastard child of the South Bank, all concrete walkways and breezeblock stairwells. You could tell where the Asians lived because of the chicken wire over the windows and letter box to stop petrol and dog shit being slipped through. It was only a matter of time before I was relieved of my records by a gang carrying knives.

This new estate looked different, most noticeably because it was made of brick, meaning it was built not constructed, but I was still intimidated by the size. I weighed it up. So it wasn't in a great location, but on the other hand there was no graffiti, no piles of rubbish and the playground looked used. A friend had driven, and we pulled up and parked.

'You don't want to do that, love, you'll get nicked,' called a woman shaking out a tablecloth on the second floor.

'Thanks!' I called up. Now *that* was a good sign.

Sara had arranged for me to see the inside of the flat as well and the caretaker pointed us towards the small block near the entrance, opposite the children's play area. We entered what could be my new home to the squeals of kids larking about on the swings, and I was knocked out and said yes immediately. It was perfect, all straight lines with huge windows – like three enormous shoeboxes made out of brick and painted cream. Built to last, it came with the kind of basics, such as built-in cupboards and decent soundproofing, that make compact living possible.

The most important feature – with both an intercom and a front door, and panic buttons (one in each room), it was safe. Safe safe safe! There were still problems – when they say unfurnished, they mean literally. I had no furniture, no cooker, no fridge and no money.

What I did have was junk mail, torrents and torrents of it. Pizzas, taxi cabs, Pentecostal newspapers and credit-card offers poured through my letter box three, four, five at a time. Have £10,000 now! 0% balance transfer! New Car Easy Credit! Would I like to buy furniture from Barney's Warehouse in 36 easy monthly payments? Would I like to sue the council if I'd slipped on the stairs, if the lights didn't work – no win no fee (these people knocked on doors too). Estate agents and letting agencies shamelessly wanted to know 'Are You Entitled to Buy Your Home?' because if you were thinking of handing your keys in, but were entitled to buy, then they'd arrange the mortgage for you (and give you £20,000 cash bonus) provided you then sold it on to them at an agreed price later.*

Guided by my mother's hand I filed these missives in the bin, and began life on a futon on the floor, with curtains donated by Sara and a friend's microwave. The first morning I woke to the unmistakable rumble of a London bus and the familiar squeak of the doors as they opened and shut. Rush hour in the main road, and I could hear it because – I'd slept with the window open! I phoned everyone, deliriously happy. 'I slept for eight hours . . . with the window open!' 'I slept for eight hours . . . with the window open!' Feeling physically safe was like getting out of debt. You don't realize what a drag it's been until it finally goes away . . .

---

* They were trying to snap up as much public housing as they could before the government changed the rules on discount.

To get furniture, I applied for a Community Care Grant, which is one of those schemes where money is passed from department to department, so Peter will loan you some money to pay for furniture, and then Paul will take it away from your benefit at a later date. They sent me a seventeen-page questionnaire, which asked not only 'What Do You Need?' but also 'Why Do You Need It?' I'd think a bed was self-explanatory. But I dutifully wrote 'To Sleep In', and moved on to my next 'need'. A table? To Eat On. And a chair? To Sit On. By the time I got to cutlery I was tempted to write 'To Make Animal Shapes' or a sofa 'To Think Deep Thoughts', but I didn't, noting instead that I was feeling the stirrings of silly, which is halfway to happy.

It took two months but my grant came through, and MIND introduced me into the world of Community furniture projects, where IKEA sofas go to die, and where you can get cookers for eighty pounds and energy-efficient fridges for fifty. For roughly three hundred quid I was able to kit my flat out with everything I needed. Sure, I looked like I was on remand, but I was incredibly grateful.

I still find the estate big – there are whole sections of it I don't know, and I might have circled the whole place twice. The block to the left is called 'The Bill' block because it's where the police are called for domestics, and every now and again youths will set fire to the bins. I once came home at 2 a.m. to discover the bins and garbage chutes ablaze, and somewhere there's a slightly hysterical 999 call of me reporting it.

'How will we know which block it's in?' said the operator.

'It's by the entrance . . .'

'Yes, but which block is it, it's a big estate.'

'There's only one entrance . . .'

'Yes, but which block?'

'You'll be able to spot it – *it's the one on fire!*'

Ten minutes later four fire engines arrived, and despite the early hour, dozens of spectators came out to watch the firefighters shimmy up ropes (the lifts' circuitry had been blown), haul up the hoses and douse the flames. They got a round of applause. Happens about twice a year.

The first week I was there my intercom buzzed and, unable to make out the voice, I peered over the balcony, to find at a young lad peering up at me.

'Yes?'

'Would you go out with a fifteen-year-old?'

'What?'

'Would you go out with a fifteen-year-old?'

Tempting though it was to hang around the swings drinking cherry brandy, I thought I'd pass.

'Bless you, sweetie, but no.'

'Wha?'

'That was a no.'

And he wandered back to his mates, no harm done.

I've been surreally heckled from the fourth floor – ''Ere, love! Are you Norwegian?' – and walked behind two black boys on their way back from school.

'You fancy Janine, you do.'

'No I don't! No I don't! No I don't! No I don't!'

'Yes you do, yes you do.'

'No man, no, what did she say?'

'She said right, she said right, she said you was *sensitive*.'

I slowly found my way around the neighbourhood, going for long aimless walks, buying milk from a different shop every day, joining the library, going to the laundrette. Had I been drinking all I'd have worked out were the pubs and the offies.

And so much for cowardly middle-class reserve, the first Christmas I had twelve cards pushed through my door from neighbours welcoming me to the estate.

It's not without its problems – that goes with a dense population. One day the police knocked on my door to explain the commotion earlier that morning, and reassure me it was over now. I'd been asleep and missed it.

'We cleared out the crack house on the second floor,' he said, 'we had to kick the door in.'

'A crack house?' I was surprised. 'I didn't know we had a crack house.'

'Yeah,' said the copper, 'as druggies go they were considerate – no loud music or nothing – it was the thieving from cars that was the problem.'

I filled in his customer user form saying yes, I understood what I'd been told, and he gave me a card in case I saw anything untoward.

We've had the odd bit of trouble with gangs, but it's not serious, and consists mostly of boys from other estates

('They're not from round here' is the common cry) trying to claim this patch.

Luckily, keeping an eye out is Louis, our multi-pierced caretaker (Louis is his vampire name), who's in his early forties, loves science fiction and *Buffy the Vampire Slayer* and is a complete joy. When I first moved he came round to fix the kitchen taps and he asked how I ended there. I told him, and he told me he'd been recently stabbed and showed me the scar. You never know what you're going to have in common with people.

It is a big place, and some might find it scary (as I did), but the difference between living on an estate and passing through, is that yes there are hoodies lurking, but if you go to the library, you'll also see hoodies working away on the computers, while keeping an eye on their baby sister.

The tenor of an estate is set by its resident alpha males, and we're lucky enough to have Dave, an Afro-Caribbean self-employed black-cab driver and amateur boxer, who loves his kids, loves his cars, and whatever you just bought, he could've got it for twenty per cent off, because his brother knows this bloke in Tottenham. We're similar ages, we both went to comprehensives and we're both self-employed – the holy grail for working people. I first noticed him cleaning his cab – which was cleaner on the outside than my flat was on the inside. 'You could eat off that,' I said, and he looked proud. Fiercely intelligent (he reads the *Independent*) and damned good-looking, he exudes energy, confidence and real-life fearlessness. When someone slashed the tyres of cars on the estate he bought plastic handcuffs and hid behind the car-park wall till two in the morning, waiting . . . if they'd turned up, he'd have taken them on, no worries. Not only do the lads know they're lads next to Dave but they want his approval. He doesn't have to throw his weight around, a simple 'Right, boys?' is enough to have them eating out of his hand.

The worst thing about living in council housing is you're all on top of each other. It's also the best thing. If anything happened to me and I screamed out of a window, fifty people would hear. I know, because I can hear them. ('Fuck off! I'm going round me mum's' . . .) The council comes and fixes things when they go wrong, the rent's reasonable and I have great neighbours (when I go away, they don't just water the plants and pick up my mail – they'll stick a pint of milk in the fridge too). For the first time in years, I loved going home. With my benefit sorted, a roof over my head, I needed something to do . . .

Chapter Thirteen

'Recalled to Life'

CHARLES DICKENS, *A TALE OF TWO CITIES*

I'D LONG AGO STOPPED telling people I was a writer, saying instead I worked for British Gas, because that way they'd never ask me, 'What's so-and-so like?' Also, it allowed people to talk to me, because I'd noticed if you write for TV, and the other person works at Boots, the focus of the conversation automatically falls on you.

I wanted something meaningful that wouldn't upset my benefit, so when Anne, my case worker at MIND, asked if I was interested in doing some volunteer work at the MIND offices I didn't hesitate to say yes. Not only were the offices within walking distance, and I'd get a free lunch, but I'd always liked odd people. First off, they've never seemed as crazy as people I was told were sane, and second, they've never done me any harm. As a teenager, I used to take the Central Line to school and would regularly see an extraordinary public-school fellow who was tall, thin, with dark hair, full lips and slightly bulbous eyes – like Michael Sheen's Tony Blair in *The Queen* –

and wore an expensive (if slightly ragged) pin-striped suit. He wouldn't stand out from the crowd, except for his habit of randomly talking out loud, and wearing a trimmed version of a Louis XIV wig.

I'd watch passengers sit next to him, then move when he started talking – sometimes subtly, sometimes not. When the train pulled into the next station, the entire carriage would engage in a collective game of who'd-sit-next-to-him-and-what-they'd-do. I'd miss my stop just to listen to his nervous chatter, all in exquisitely unfashionable English, about his family, and a friend of his aunt Bertha's called Mavis, who kept popping by unannounced . . . 'I don't know where she was from, but wherever limbs are heavy and breasts are large – that's the place!'

Genius. I came across him in Regent's Park being tormented by some teenage French day-trippers. I chased them away with my umbrella, emboldened by their obvious wealth (I am very rarely the hardest one there), and then took his arm.

'Thank you, thank you, dear thing,' he stuttered. 'Wretched boys – not a clever one among them.' I saw him a few times after that, but never spoke to him again.

Whether or not he was genuinely ill as opposed to, for example, eccentric is impossible to say. Mental illness is hard to define. Schizophrenia, bipolar disorder and psychopathy (once called split personality, manic depression and nutjob) aren't like smallpox or diphtheria, they're labels (and even that word is emotive) used by doctors for people displaying groups of symptoms. None of this means that mental illness doesn't exist, people can and do get ill, rather that it's a broad spectrum that has at its centre a shifting and nebulous notion of 'within normal range'.

I started on reception, armed with numbers for the crisis lines and drop-in centres, a helpful disposition and their Big Book of Drugs. For a number of reasons, people often don't understand what's been prescribed for them; sometimes it's not explained, or they're too distressed to absorb what they're told. Before the Web, there were scant resources for people who wanted information about something that would affect their brain – that is to say, the very essence of themselves.

All drugs have side effects. The SSRI the psychologist put me on was loathsome to me but effective for others, whereas amitriptyline, an old-fashioned tri-cyclic antidepressant, worked wonderfully for me. It didn't whack a smile on my face and there was no euphoria, but it helped me sleep and eat, which aided concentration and made me feel better, thus lifting my mood. I asked my GP why this worked and others hadn't. He admitted they weren't sure.

Looking it up in MIND's big book I discovered it was also a treatment for a bewildering number of ailments including irritable-bowel syndrome, migraines and vaginal swelling, bed wetting and chronic pain, chronic cough, interstitial cystitis and male chronic pelvic-pain syndrome, to name but a few. I suddenly felt very covered.

There are six main types of drugs for mental illness,

antidepressants (self-explanatory), stimulants (as seen on *Desperate Housewives*), antipsychotics (can be very strong and sometimes called 'the liquid cosh') for schizophrenia and mania, mood stabilizers for things like bipolar disorder, anxiolytics for anxiety disorders and finally the depressants such as sedatives and anaesthetics. Several times a day bewildered people would phone and say they'd been prescribed (they'd read it slowly off a label) 'Me . . . sor . . . id . . . azine', or 'Pro . . . m . . . azine', and you'd look it up and try to explain it to them in everyday language. Psychiatric medication is a medical minefield, and there are dozens of different strands of thinking, but MIND's policy was *never* to advise callers not to take their medication, but to operate an open-door policy on information. Some callers would ask my advice, and I'd tell them my only regret re. anti-depressants was not taking them sooner.

Calls came from anybody. The lonely would just want a chat. Others wanted us to section someone (usually a neighbour) and I'd have to explain that wasn't within our remit. The most difficult calls were when you had an opinion but weren't qualified to say. A woman phoned aggressively demanding therapy for her son (aged seven) who, she said, was causing problems at home. Her fantastic new boyfriend had moved in and the son was taking it badly and 'ruining it' for the rest of them. I resisted talking about scapegoating and said family therapists usually liked to see the whole family. 'The others are fine,' she said, 'it's just him.' 'Nevertheless,' I started, 'it's rare that one child is the sole cause of—' and she cut me off with, 'Well, if you're not going to help!' and hung up.

I liked going to the office, and I admired the staff, who did their best to help the sometimes unhelpable. People like their victims to be doe-eyed and barefoot, and the mentally unwell are rarely that. After a few months I began to know my way around the system. Who could help with benefits? What about employment rights? What charities offered what help with housing? Who did therapy on a sliding scale?

Eventually I progressed from reception to teaching computing. I've always liked computers; I'm not a Luddite, but I'm not a geek either. The MINDWORKS programme was there to teach basic computing to people with mental-health problems, to help them get back to work. (Only not really – mental health is so underfunded you have to say things like that to get money out of the government. You can't say, 'It reduces isolation,' or 'It encourages independence,' or even 'It's fun.')

There were three of us in MINDWORKS and I was very much the junior (having been taught by the other two), but it was more about the clients than us, and they fell into two distinct categories – locals and asylum-seekers.

At the time, London's social services were in crisis, having been caught short by the arrival of refugees from some of the nastiest war zones in the world, who if not crazy on arrival were soon pushed over the edge by being locked up as criminals in detention centres with no end in sight. These were men, women and children who'd escaped from places such as Rwanda and the Congo (always the Congo) but who weren't quite damaged enough to qualify for help from Helen Bamber's Medical Foundation for the Victims of Torture, and so were left to the mercies of local boroughs and charities.

My first day saw a commotion in reception. Two people from child social services had turned up looking for a woman who MIND was helping to secure a college placement. They'd had a report she'd been locking her two-year-old in the flat and leaving it there, all day, on its own. When challenged the woman cursed and flailed. She didn't understand *why* these fools didn't just leave her be – 'Go away! Go away!' she said and refused to talk to them. But of course they couldn't leave, so they phoned the police . . . When they arrived, the sight of uniforms didn't help. And so on.

It took half a dozen people half a dozen hours to sort out a problem that started a thousand miles away under a different sun.

The woman was from Sierra Leone. One day she went to see her sister, who'd married a man in a neighbouring village. Leaving behind her six children but taking her baby on her back because it would need feeding, she walked two days to her sister's village, to find every man, woman and child had been macheted to death, the bits tumbled together into a bloody mound in the open. Terrified, she ran back to her village, to discover that the rebel army had beaten her to it. Her children, husband, parents, aunts, uncles, cousins, all butchered. No one in two villages left alive, save her and her baby. As far as she was concerned her baby was safer in a locked flat than it had ever been – no men were going to break down the door with machetes.

MIND's job was to help bridge the two worlds, and they did it astonishingly well. We knew our clients had been screened, as much for their protection as for ours, but apart from that we made a point of not knowing their history, medical or otherwise. They were 'Patrick' and you were 'Abi'. Often you were the first middle-class white person they'd met who wasn't a lawyer or a doctor – who didn't have power over them (we called it 'grab 'n' jab'). Just asking them if they'd like a cup of tea could be transformational.

They wanted to know the basics. How to go on-line, set up an email account and write a letter. Simple inclusive lessons. Teaching them how to surf the Web was the most fun, even in dial-up days. Watching men and women who'd been culturally dislocated discover newspapers and websites written in their own language was magical. A Nigerian man told me with a sheepish smile, he read a paper he'd be ashamed to be seen with at home – 'It is exceedingly stupid' – just because he could. They were all kind, considerate and wounded. It could take weeks to break down the timidity, reassuring grown men that they didn't need to put their hand up to go to the toilet, they didn't need to call you Miss or keep saying thank you, and these weren't allowances, it was fine. ('Thank you.')

Some, as a mark of trust, would tell you what they used to do – running a radio-repair shop, or driving a cab. It was as if they wanted to explain that the person they were now was the result of what had happened to them, not who they really were. Others were silent as if they had no past. Doubly shunned, as immigrants and mental-health sufferers, all had a fervent desire to improve themselves and most spoke at least three languages. A young Moroccan boy gave me an English version of the Koran and called me Westminster Abbey, laughing splendidly at his own pun. Seeing him able to make jokes in another language, not yet eighteen and a refugee, was genuinely cheering.

On the estate, despite being the posh bird who picked up litter, I was also, noticeably, a white Londoner. Going to and fro, chatting in the post office, you got to know people, and with Londoners, once you'd gone through the regulation 'Where are you from?' (or 'Who do you support?') and heard 'Shepherds Bush' (and 'QPR') it was as if a key has been turned. Now they were free to tell you about how great the estate was 'before all the shit' got dumped here. It wasn't everybody, and it wasn't even said maliciously, more in the tone you'd use to complain about the weather. Their environment was changing and they hadn't been consulted.

I knew from the police that an Eritrean woman in the main block had been subject to a racist attack, and I noticed the 'headscarves' didn't dawdle. When they walked, pushing prams or carrying shopping, they went from A to B. The flat opposite mine had a steady flow of asylum-seekers (it was privately owned and rented back by the local authority) and I used to wonder about the people. To a man with a hammer every problem looks like a nail and to me everything looks like a story. One Arab family was there for about six weeks. The father was tall, maybe six foot five, slightly stooped as if in semi-supplication and wearing a shabby tweed jacket. The mother (unscarved) was about my age, and together they had a teenager, a ten-year-old and a toddler. I imagined he was a doctor, or a professor, he had that air about him, quietly spoken and self-effacing. Leaving one day I noticed them behind me. Holding the door, as is polite, each and every one (including the toddler) stopped and said thank you with a small bow.

But misfortune is promiscuous and you don't need a military junta or machete-wielding madman to break someone's spirit. We saw many casualties of the new target-led workplace, ground down by staff cutbacks, ever-increasing workloads and bullying management – good people made to feel useless until they finally broke down. For manual workers, there were industrial accidents – one young man's dream of being a guitarist ended when he was shoved onto a youth training scheme which was so poorly run that his upper left arm, from biceps to elbow, was crushed flat by a forklift truck.*

---

* These clients often wanted to talk about what had happened. Listening was as important as teaching.

I worked with a seventeen-year-old who was raising two kids on her own despite looking barely fifteen. Genuinely beautiful with curly black hair, brown skin and a sweet smile, you could have put a woolly hat on her and stuck her in a Benetton ad. But everything suggested was met by an immediate response of 'I can't do that, I'm too stupid.' 'Would you like to type a letter?' Type? 'I can't do that, I'm too stupid.' 'How about go on-line?' 'Nah, I can't do that, I'm too stupid.' 'How about create a new file?' 'I can't do that . . .' and she'd giggle and shuffle her feet. I don't know what happened to her, only that I felt an overwhelming urge to reach back into her past, find out who'd told this perfectly nice young woman that she was stupid and beat the crap out of them.

I might have been doing the teaching, but they were doing the educating. I began to feel a renewed sense of good fortune in comparison. Not simply because I hadn't escaped from a war zone, but because I was thin, white, pretty, literate and had lots of nice caring friends. I don't say that as a boast – but as a dawning recognition. True social advantages are things that work for you whether you chose them or not.

I liked feeling useful and being praised doubly. I was clean and sober, happily housed, enjoying my work and my confidence was growing. I hadn't thought about my career, who I used to be, for an age. This was my life now, and it suited me. With that in mind, I decided to try therapy one last time, and using all the resources at MIND's disposal, I finally found a place and a person that worked.

Chapter Fourteen

Small cares have many words, big cares have few.

SENECA

THERAPY IS AN ODD BEAST. Like 'exercise' or 'work', the word itself is a blanket term that doesn't describe what it involves, but merely categorizes what it is – something that attempts to cure. Years before I'd seen a Freudian psychiatrist and duly lay on a couch staring at a blank wall, with my therapist sat behind me in a chair, until I read that Freud only put his patients on a couch facing away from him so they couldn't see him ('I cannot put up with being stared at by other people for eight hours a day,' he said), which didn't strike me as a particularly therapeutic principle. It made me feel disconnected from the process, and coupled with my therapist's determination to read meaning into abstract things – which I suppose goes with the territory – I just couldn't shake the feeling that it was astrology trying to pass itself off as astronomy at fifty pounds an hour.

I'm not sure if I'm bad at emotion or just not that sensitive. I tend to feel things retrospectively, and realize 'I was cross' or 'That upset me' only weeks, sometimes years, after the event. I know I'm not spiritual. I have friends who're comforted by the idea of a higher power, but having prayed as an experiment – fifteen minutes every day for a year and never having got past the idea I was talking to myself – I agree with Darwin: the world is pretty much as one would expect 'if there is, at bottom, no design, no purpose, no evil, no good, nothing but blind, pitiless indifference'. I actually find this heart-warming. I like the idea I'm not that important. It's restful.

But I'd got a lot out of my CBT sessions and I knew from experience that problems don't disappear, but transmute, and gifted as I was at avoiding things, I was sure keeping real life in abeyance would lead to a reckoning somewhere down the line. If nothing else I didn't want to be poor, which meant I needed work, but I had no idea what to do – it wasn't like I had a degree to fall back on, and it's safe to say I was looking at a blank future. Which isn't always a bad thing. I wasn't a mother, with kids relying on me, I was housed, had enough to eat and I was feeling steady. Better still, I hadn't had a traumatic attack for months. So I ploughed through lists of therapists offering sliding scales, but even six pounds per session was still ten per cent of my income. Eventually I found an organization that offered free counselling to those on low incomes by using the patients (or 'clients' as we became in the new parlance) as guinea pigs for trainee counsellors – like the cut-price haircuts you get as a 'model'.

Bizarrely for an organization dedicated to helping poor people, the offices were on Bishopsgate* in the City, just a hundred and fifty yards from the brand-new chrome-and-glass Royal Bank of Scotland building. Tucked into a crumbling old house with a wiggly staircase and uneven floors, the offices backed onto a dark thin alleyway – and you could move from Wall Street to Dickens and back again just by walking around the block.

After attending a psychological evaluation and passing the audition, I signed a contract promising to turn up one evening a week for a year. My first session was in December and I trudged past the bars packed with suits and skirts quaffing G&T and three-quid bottles of imported beer, and the homeless people tucked into doorways with a dog and a hat, and was buzzed in to meet my counsellor for the first time.

Late thirties, Afro-Caribbean, with elegantly short hair, big earrings and a dark blue polo-neck jumper, Claire projected a wonderful balance of kindness and competence and was effortlessly happier than me. I knew she was changing careers (hence the evening sessions) but she wouldn't tell me what she did (Come on, you're a teacher, aren't you?) and spurned my curiosity with a winning smile. I liked her immediately.

'Our' room was a cubicle on the second floor, and looked like it had been kitted with furniture stolen from

<hr>

* Over forty-six thousand people work in Bishopsgate, but it has a resident population of only forty-eight.

a community centre in the eighties. We sat down and Claire produced a box of tissues ('That's ominous,' I said), placed it on the table between us and we began.

Talking cures are just that. You talk. There's no activity, and in this room, no pacing about either. Sitting still for an hour is a challenge for me at the best of times, and if you want someone to wander off-subject I'm your gal. But as Claire pointed out after our first few uneventful sessions, I must have wanted to be there, because it took a lot of effort. Why not use the time productively?

Interestingly, being sexually assaulted didn't come up at first. It was important but it wasn't urgent. My failed relationship was causing the most immediate pain, followed by family, money and work. So I wailed about the ex and got that out of the way. Then after the hors d'oeuvres came the meat – the family. When people ask us about our childhoods, we know they're asking, 'What are you really like?' which is why many of us are cagey. But however inadequate we feel as adults, as Alfred Adler pointed out, the only way to be happy is to have had happy parents. The rest of us are playing catch-up.

In my experience with Claire, catch-up consisted of piecing things together and constructing the bigger picture. For example, a huge issue that had dogged me for years was why my mother stayed with my father. I was indignant that a clever woman was able to ignore what was going on in front of her eyes, sacrificing her children's well-being to preserve – what? Didn't it occur to her that raising children in a house where there was more hard-core pornography than literature (and by God we had a lot of books) might not be healthy? Didn't she notice his inappropriate comments about me and my friends during puberty, such as, 'I've just noticed, you're growing up,' staring at my developing breasts, and 'Rachael's coming on nicely.' (There's a reason I stopped having my friends over.) Didn't she notice him baiting women, whispering things like, 'Do you shave? And I don't mean your legs,' into their ears and chuckling at their unease?

'Why don't you wear a nice frock?' Granny used to say.

'Because I don't want my father looking at me,' was what I didn't say.

Worst of all, couldn't she see that his bullying Harriet was a deliberate strategy to quell his inappropriate desire towards her?

But now I was in bigger-picture territory, and the bigger the picture the fewer the guilty parties. Talking to Claire I remembered a conversation I had about Charlie Chaplin when I was twelve years old. 'I don't like his drunk act,' I told Mum, having just seen some of his films on BBC2. 'I know,' she said fixedly. 'Drunks aren't funny, not funny at all. They're sick.' I meant I preferred Buster Keaton, but she meant something else. I remembered, too, when there was a proposal to incorporate child benefit into other benefits, and my mother was stoutly against it. It had to be paid to the mother, she said repeatedly, 'otherwise the husbands might drink it away'. Because our house had so much alcohol in it – we even had a still in the kitchen for homemade wine – it wasn't until sitting with Claire that I pieced it together. Her father was a drunk! D'oh! That's why he died young, never fought in the war, was never, ever mentioned (I don't know his name). It also explains why alcoholism doesn't just run in our family, it gallops. So, my mother was sent off to be raised by an institution and then like co-dependants everywhere went out and married her father – a distant moody alpha male – and tried to control his addictions. She managed to keep a lid on his drinking, but his porn use was beyond her.

Getting to the place where you see your parents as human beings rather than simply as connected to you is humbling. Prior to this it had never occurred to me that she might have been lonely, with her husband spending hours in his office every night looking at porn filled with pictures of women the age of her daughter, while she read Elizabeth Gaskell in the lounge. She didn't come from a generation where you talked things out, or sought professional help – she was 'pull yourself together and find something useful or self-improving to do'. She did the best she could. She fed us, taught us to read and prayed (literally, she found God just before she died) everything would be all right.

And what of my father? I'd imagined there was a dark trauma in his past, a crisis that would explain everything. But shortly after I broke off contact, a delightful cousin called Trudy popped up from down under (as Anzacs often do) and revealed over lunch that Dad's family home in Lower Hutt was the happiest in the street – it was full of laughter and his mother Tude was a mother to everyone. Trudy confirmed what I'd long suspected, that Dad was mixed-race – Tude is a Maori name and Dad looked Maori, wore a greenstone Hei-Tiki on a silver chain his whole life and even slept with an ornate Maori war club attached to the wall above his head. I can't believe he was ashamed of this because we were always given a positive impression of Maoris and told gleefully how when the white settlers arrived there was no 'Welcome to our island, please take our women' from them, indeed they distinguished themselves from many native peoples by determinedly beating the crap out of the first colonists. I remembered a minor brou-hah-hah he caused at a dinner party. A man was waffling on about immigrants. 'You got a problem with immigrants?' said Dad, shifting from advertising man to Maori prop forward. 'Uh, no, no,' said the man, looking even whiter and correcting himself.

So where did it come from, this desire to crush, to see his son as a threat, rather than feel proud that he'd fathered such an intelligent, creative child? Why couldn't he enjoy Harriet's bright-eyed playfulness and unstoppable kindness? She was a champion swimmer and he didn't watch a single race. It seems unnatural. Had he led a rambunctious playboy lifestyle that would be one thing. But he lived a depressing and for the most part lonely life. He wanted women but they were repelled by him. He tried to be one of the men, but they didn't want him either. After forty years in the country he didn't have one close friend.

It's difficult to feel any sympathy with a bully, and I

can't say my feelings shifted – you need warm memories for that, and I had few. But maybe some understanding crept in. If my father had wanted help, who could he have gone to? Men are rubbish at admitting things are wrong and have a terrible record of self-care, so how much harder to admit that something like their porn use is out of control. Even twenty years later, sympathy is scarce and mention of sex addiction or Sex Addicts Anonymous is mainly confined to sniggering at celebrities falling from grace. It took me over a year to find therapy and I was highly motivated, and had time on my hands. Too often with men's health issues, intervention only kicks in after a crisis.

Claire was a great support during these difficult weeks. Girls are conditioned not to get angry, so it was a real struggle to let it out in public. Similarly with crying: I hate looking pathetic when there's someone watching, but week after week, I'd leave the session, return home and flop onto the bed so wiped I could barely move.

I saw my siblings anew in Carton's '*airy galleries from which the loves and graces looked upon him, gardens in which the fruits of life hung ripening*' and imagined how they could've been. Harriet a dancer, or a doctor, or social worker, she loved helping people. And Mark, a photographer maybe – he had a good eye but lacked the courage to pursue it – or possibly an academic – he was after all the clever one. To inherit a proclivity for self-harm along with genuine talent seemed terribly unfair. It takes so little to hamstring a soul – not damage it irreparably, but just enough to ensure that it makes crappy decisions in all the areas that count.

I was angry at myself for chastising them for not giving me support when it was clear they couldn't emotionally support themselves. Never trust a naked man if he offers to lend you his shirt, as the old African saying goes. Our family was not built for trauma – dull tragedy, maybe, but the shock of my being attacked applied a pressure it simply couldn't take. And that wasn't their fault.

The man who attacked me lurked in the corners of my conversation, but lacked identity and form – he had no bigger picture. He was a random event, like a nightmare inversion of winning the Lottery. It was a million-to-one shot, and I was just that unlucky.

My own self-dissection was rather bloody but at least short. We all get to the stage where we have to own up to who we are, rather than cling to who we'd like to be – but I had hoped it would be later. I said to a close friend while in Starbucks, in what I imagined to be a revelation, that I thought I was 'a bit moody' and she laughed so hard coffee came out of her nose. Apparently everyone else knew. I also discovered I'm overbearing, pedantic, argumentative, with a tendency to feel emotions in block colours – angry, sad, happy, etc. – like a Mondrian painting rather than the elegant Degas I'd assumed was my inner palette. But I also learned that I was a fighter, and came to believe if I kept on going something good would happen, I just didn't know what.

The sad thing about my year with Claire is that it came

to an abrupt halt. I often wonder what became of her, but I'm certain wherever she is and whatever she's doing, she's doing it incredibly well. As journeys go I'd covered a lot of ground, and made one final discovery. The opposite of depression is not happiness, it's vitality, and vitality drives you forward. And for the first time in a good way, the rest was silence.

Chapter Fifteen

'Good friends, good books and a sleepy
conscience: this is the ideal life.'

MARK TWAIN

IT TOOK A LONG WHILE to settle down after therapy,
so I decided, with time on my hands, to re-apply for
Criminal Injuries. At first I was turned down because I'd
left it too late (there's a two-year cut-off – 'It has been
decided that there are no particular circumstances to allow
the time limit to be waived in this case'). Didn't stop me.
Everyone gets turned down for *everything* first time.

They said I could appeal in writing (using the enclosed
form), and not for the first time I realized how good it
was not to be intimidated by words. (One day, though,
I'll stand and shake my paw at the heavens, swearing, as
God is my witness, I'll never fill in another form again.)

The system wavered and conceded I might have a legitimate claim, but they needed buckets of information.
First and most importantly my crime reference number.

That meant calling the police and I felt a bit squirrelly
('Hello, you won't remember me, but . . .'). People had

often asked me over the years 'Did they catch him?' and I had to admit I didn't know. What I didn't tell them is that I'd never tried to find out, and since the *Crimewatch* interview had had no contact with the police. He might've been in prison for all I knew. There's no legal requirement for the police to tell victims if they've caught a perpetrator, unless they victim is needed to give evidence in court. If the case were a 'TIC' (Taken Into Consideration), which has been used by forces to help clear their books, then they wouldn't need the victim at all and the crime would just be marked off . . .

With some trepidation I called Stoke Newington police station. I asked to be put through to their sexual-violence unit, where I explained who I was and what I needed. The detective sent someone off to look up the file. Someone at the station remembered my case, and it didn't take long for them to find it. The detective told me the case was still open, and no they hadn't caught him. I asked if he might still be prowling the neighbourhood. The detective covered the receiver ('Geoff,' he called, 'how many rapists we got working this patch?' 'Three,' came the reply) and told me he might still be active, but there was no way of knowing. He gave me my crime reference number ('Major Crime 77' property reference number Book 66, no. 14/1993) and I had the first piece of paperwork for my claim.

I had to jump through a few hoops, and cover them in sick notes from doctors and shrinks, but I did of course have a complete file proving I was bonkers from my housing quest, and to my complete joy, they said yes. My sum was calculated as follows . . .

AWARD FROM INJURY UNDER
THE TARIFF SCHEME

Injury Description	Band	Amount
Mental disorder (over 1 year)	12	£7,500

AWARD FOR PAST AND
FUTURE FINANCIAL LOSS

Description	Paragraph	Amount
Lump sum payment	33	£4,000

Total award payable – £9,625

It was only when writing this that I looked at the covering letter closely, and realized there's no mention of rape, or sexual assault, or physical injury. I completely missed this:

having considered the medical reports obtained by the Authority, it is considered you were suffering from a pre-existing medical condition. A full award is therefore considered inappropriate, and the award is therefore reduced by 25 per cent.

They were no details of what I had that was worth 25 per cent off. Rape victims have been docked money for all sorts of reasons, most notoriously for 'contributing' to their own attack by having a drink. I called the CICB and asked them what this meant, but they apologized and said they hadn't kept records.

After the 'Deduction in respect of exacerbation of - £1,875' my total injury award was £5,625. Loss of earning brought it up to £9,625. It might not sound much, but remember that to an impoverished person £17.63 is a fortune.

If I was attacked now, I would be awarded more, under the Criminal Injuries Compensation Scheme 2008. The new CICB website is user-friendly yet still as diabolically persnickety. For example, if a criminal cut off your arm, you'd get £55,000 for a 'dominant arm' but only £33,000 'non-dominant arm', with the caveat that 'if there is no remaining arm/hand with any useful function' then it would shoot up to £82,000. (If he cut off both arms, they'd pony up a straight £110,000.)

The sexual-assault categories have been refined, but the sums seem paltry, and leave you uneasily wondering, how exactly did they tabulate this? The rates are . . .

- Minor – non-penetrative sexual physical act/or acts over clothing £1,000
- Serious – non-penetrative sexual physical act/or acts under clothing £2,000
- Severe – non-penile penetrative and/or oral-genital act or acts £3,300
- Non-consensual penile penetration of the vagina and/

or anus and/or mouth by one attacker £11,000 By two
or more attackers £13,500
– Resulting in serious internal bodily injuries £22,000
    With an additional page on 'disabling mental illness'
ranging from moderate (£22,000) to severe (£44,000).

But I was in no mood to complain – I was busy being
delighted. The first thing I did was buy some nice IKEA
blinds, replace some of my shabbier furniture and buy a
second-hand washing machine. Next to passing my driving test, nothing has made me happier than owning my
own washing machine. I ran it almost continuously for
three days. When that buzz wore off, I bought myself a
tool of my old trade. A brand spanking new iMac, which
I called Baby, because it was mine, all mine. With a brand-
new second-hand TV, I was starting to feel more me
again. The rest I put into the Post Office for emergencies
and carried on.

One very normal council-flat day, a year after I started at
MIND, I was looking out of the window, nursing a cup
of tea, as kids played loudly on the estate. Something
struck me, a strange feeling I couldn't quite place. Therapy
training kicked in. I took a moment to sit with it.
Hmmmm. I realized I was, in that second . . . happy.

Not the cartwheel happiness of a first night, young love
or sunny day. This was warm contentment. If this was as
good as life got, then that was fine by me. A most peculiar

feeling – not drug-inspired, no one else was involved; not praise or money. Just an incalculable sense of well-being. And of being free.

Unbidden, 1979 bubbled into my brain. I've always liked autobiographies that begin, 'It was 1941, Germany was advancing across Europe and in London bombs were falling. Somewhere in Suffolk a boy was born . . .' 1979 was a big year. British history will remember it for Thatcher taking power. I'll remember it as the Year When Everyone Left Me Alone. Until then I'd never really appreciated the upside to benign neglect.

The teachers were bricking it about their jobs, so their attention to detail fell off, and with a sister in a mental hospital I had a rock-solid excuse for not being in lessons – 'I was visiting, sir.' Course, no one ever offered to take me, and I knew not to ask. But hey, an excuse is an excuse. The bullies who'd been having a field day for three years, mashing me for being clever, gay, posh, a book-reader, realized that having failed to protect me, I now had as much contempt for the teachers as for them ('I'm sorry, sir, I just have to go somewhere more interesting . . .') and left me alone. (Mind, I'd gone from straight As to C–, so it's fair to say their work here was done.)

Politics was everywhere. The BNP and their Harrington-jacketed boot boys hung around our school gates and after a series of IRA bombs went off, Irish class mates received threatening phone calls from men promising to 'get you Paddy fuckers', while on the other side of the fence a Protestant Irish friend and her family were hiding from the Provos because her stepdad had written a book about the British army in Ireland.

I made a pact with the teachers that I'd keep up with coursework if they didn't hassle me about non-attendance, and being one of only a handful of pupils expected to get any grades, and with ILEA (Inner London Education Authority) under threat, I was in a good bargaining position. Every morning I got on the bus and felt a tingle as I passed my stop, and every minute it took me further and further away from school. With a junior buss pass, you could get to the West End for 10p, and the world, as Arthur Daley put it, was my lobster. Because the old post-war cross-party coalition hadn't broken down, all sorts of things like museums and art galleries were still free. I'd regularly pop into the National Gallery and spend hours parked in front of Holbein's *The Ambassadors** watching people bend down to see the trompe-l'œil (the squidged-up skull reminding us that even the powerful are mortal) and following tour guides at a distance – close enough to hear what was being said, not so close as to have to pay.

On Wednesdays and Thursdays there were matinees and my carefully honed sidling skills came into their own – I'd find a show having an interval, slip my coat into my bag and join the people milling around in the lobby, then follow a couple (elderly tourists were your best bet) back into the auditorium. The knack was looking as if you'd been there for hours, not just arrived, which meant

* http://en.wikipedia.org/wiki/The_Ambassadors_(Holbein).

slowing your breathing and slouching, slightly bored – like in a meeting or a maths class.

Many days were spent joining in with the demonstrations outside the South African Embassy in Trafalgar Square. I met Desmond Tutu once. 'They think we are trying to chase the white man into the ocean. We are not trying to chase the white man into the ocean. However,' he said with a wicked smile, 'if he wants to jump, we are not going to stop him . . .' I wasn't averse to shoplifting or scoffing the odd pizza and leaving before the bill. The rest of the time I wandered the streets in a delicious daze, taking it all in. Bliss was it in that dawn to be alive, but to be young was very heaven. I said to a fellow writer once, 'Didn't you bunk off and have a look?' 'Abi,' he sighed, 'I lived in Leicester.'*

If I felt the need for family, I dropped round my Afro-Caribbean friends' houses, where I was confounded by the raised voices, open displays of affection and the front room you weren't allowed into. Apart from 'hot comb'† day (when it smelt like someone was roasting a badger) I'd never been happier around people who were related. For company I hung around with my fellow readers and Tony, a black boy in my class, who, in the days when it was acceptable to question whether a black boy, sorry, a West Indian boy, could play for England, carried around

---

* Sorry, Leicester.
† Ye olde hair-straighteners – medieval lumps of metal, heated up and pulled through the curls to make them ready for church.

a thick black felt pen so when he came across National Front graffiti (always an NF) he could amend it thus:

NF O R E V E R
I
G
G
E
R
S

Once I started an evening job at a local arts theatre (working in the kitchen), I found I could go days without meeting an adult with any authority over me. By the time I left school my ambitions had been reduced to never wanting to get up before ten and never calling anyone sir unless I wanted to. A lifetime later, I finally had that freedom. Once the state kicks in, it kicks in solid. You don't have to send it a birthday card or remember its kids' names and it never guilt-trips you into calling ('I waited in all day'). Nanny state – yes, please. I ate decent food, kept my flat clean and behaved in a neighbourly fashion and my rent, poll tax and national insurance were all paid.

Doctors were attentive, friends were pleased and the only people I wanted to know where I was had my address. Lacking an agent proper, I wasn't even up for work, and apart from helping pals with Edinburgh shows, no one expected anything. On sunny days I'd hop the Tube to St Paul's Cathedral and stand dead centre under the dome, with the shafts of sunlight cutting through the church as Wren intended. It's one of the still points of the universe, one of the most perfect shots in the world, taking hundreds of men over thirty years to set up and it's there at the end of a Tube ride. I didn't bunk into any plays – I'm not as good at blending in now, and I would've felt guilty. However, once you've paid to see one film in a multiplex, it doesn't hurt if you slip in and see what else is on. I wasn't so much filling my mind as emptying it of misery, self-pity, anger and desire. I was incredibly grateful, I knew my thriving was because decades earlier people had decided no one should be allowed to slip through the cracks because of misfortune.

With my mind a great deal improved, I decided to delve further into the goodwill of the state, and give my body another look. My nose was the main problem. Since it had been squished, my sinuses responded to air pressure like a barometer, inducing terrible migraines and leaving me begging for rain. With money being pumped into the NHS, my doctor sent me to a consultant and sixteen weeks later I had a date for my operation which was so fast it was almost frightening. But the nurses in the X-ray department were excellent, and, having stuck my head in a big machine that went kerlunk kerlunk kerlunk while they hid behind a screen, let me see what they'd recorded. Looking at an X-ray of your own head is childishly fascinating. Like seeing the back of your head only more so.

The surgery required an overnight stay at the Royal

National Ear, Nose & Throat Hospital in Gray's Inn Road. Things went smoothly, but when I came to, I felt as if my head had been hollowed out and stuffed. I noticed a blue string dangling from either nostril. I tentatively tugged one and a nurse, seeing I was awake, came over. 'Leave the tampons,' she said, 'they're stopping the blood.'

I've woken up in some rum states after drinking, but never with a Lillet up each nostril. Later, accompanied by a burst of blood, they were gently removed, my stitches checked, new stuffing inserted and bandages applied, and I was judged good to go home.

That next day was, as the news kept telling us, the hottest day in Britain since records began and as I lay sweltering on my bed, head pounding, cheek and sinuses aching, I resolved that in future, should an elephant sit on my head, I'd just learn to live with it. Why anyone would put themselves through this just to look good is beyond me.

However, once the swelling went down I was delighted to notice the vast improvement in my breathing, even if I had been left with a hole in my septum that means I can wear a little piggy nose ring without piercing.

I was having a great time not working, and despite my lovely new iMac, hadn't felt compelled to write a word for ages. I'd never written things down so I'd remember them because I always remembered them, and I've never written for fun because it isn't. Writing was never a long-term ambition, or even a short one. 'No man but a blockhead ever wrote except for money,' said Samuel Johnson and I agree. Like acting, it's not so much difficult as stressful – trying not to be rubbish is demanding, and I'd much rather have been a painter, a footballer or a marine biologist, but they require training and talent (and in the case of football a change of gender). Plus, I've known for years I'm not ambitious, I'm competitive – wild horses couldn't get me to a party because important people were there, but any self-respecting ten-year-old can still get me with 'race you to that tree' (and don't think I'd let them win). I don't have the attention span to be materially possessive. People have flown me to some remarkable places over the years, and I've noticed that after three days, even having a quad bike and your own beach gets samey. Only ideas and stories have staying power, and thinking them is enough, you don't need to write them down. That's like homework.

So I wasn't yearning to get back into the saddle. I was happy being happy. I no longer had a writing agent, but I did have a script-editing agent (and friend) who every now and again would offer me the odd job. Around this time he called. 'Would you like to script-edit *Thomas the Tank Engine*?'

Chapter Sixteen

'Children have more need of
models than of critics'

JOSEPH JOUBERT

WHEN PEOPLE DISCOVER I've written *Thomas*, they
always ask if I've got children and when I say no, don't
know whether to commiserate or congratulate me. I
wanted kids when I was in my early twenties, and Simon
was the closest I'd ever come to thinking maybe. But it's
fair to say since I was attacked, I'd other things on my
mind.

I've always enjoyed children and have found that like
adults, they're as interesting as the questions you put to
them. If you ask a seven-year-old, 'How was your day at
school?' you'll get a pretty dull reply, but if you grab a
box of crayons and ask, 'How can we make a dog fly?',
'What do you think the world would look like if it were
run by cats?' or 'What would you rather be, a premiership
footballer or invisible?' as long as they're not questions
with a wrong or right answer, you'll have a grand time.
When it comes to storytelling for children, you don't need

to have kids, you have to remember what it was like to be a kid, and on that account I was safe. But I wasn't entirely sure I was ready to be back in the real world. I liked welfare. It was both worry- and work-free, and if I gave it all up and it didn't work out I'd be stuffed. The contract was for eight weeks and required a daily commute to Shepperton Studios (a fabled name from the screen credits), a good two hours away.

It was thinking of the folks at MIND that caused me to say yes. If this wasn't an opportunity then I don't know what was and I felt obliged to give it a go. I phoned the DSS. I knew I had to 'tell us immediately', sorry, *TELL US IMMEDIATELY* if my circumstances changed. It took me ten minutes to get through.

'Name, address and National Insurance number...' said the operator in Glasgow (the branch of the DSS dealing with incapacity benefit was in Scotland). 'How can I help you?'

'I want to come off incapacity benefit.'

'You what?' said the woman as if she hadn't heard properly.

'I want to come off incapacity benefit.'

'Am I hearing you right?'

'I want to come off incapacity benefit,' I said, starting to think there was an accent barrier.

'You're saying you want to come off incapacity benefit?'

'This doesn't happen much, does it?' I said. She laughed.

The deed was done. I was back on my own two feet. I had no idea what I was taking on.

Shepperton looked like the US film studios you see on TV, only stuck in a 1950s time warp with peeling paint, an old-style works canteen and no central heating. Once a cornerstone of the British film industry, it's suffered all the vagaries of that industry, and was in the hands of the banks until Ridley and Tony Scott (of *Blade Runner* and *Top Gun* fame) put a consortium together to save it. Some of the sound stages are as gigantic as aircraft hangars, with curved roofs and vast doors, high enough to drive a double-decker bus in. Others like the *Thomas* stages were smaller and more intimate. After arriving and taking up position in the office adjacent to the producer, I was brought up to speed. It was a very bad speed. Had I known this speed even existed, I might very well have stayed at home. The then management (long since gone) had decided that *Thomas* was a simple show, and therefore didn't need professional writers and so had hired students to write it on the cheap, ending up with fifteen scripts of varying lengths, in different styles, and filming was booked to start the week after next.

That set the tone for the management. When I visited the workshops, where the engines were made, I discovered the noticeboard was like one in a garage. Titty cartoons, Arab jokes, Eastern European jokes ('What do you call a Serbian prostitute with no teeth?' 'Slobonmydickyou-bitch') and I made a breathlessly unpopular start when I told the producer to take it down. And I mean told him,

I didn't ask. Things only got better with the crew when I turned new scripts around, fast enough to keep everyone in their jobs. But as the only woman on the production team, it was initially a lonely cold place to work. Contrary to the management's asinine assumption, *Thomas* is one of the hardest kids' shows to write, because its leads can't actually do anything. Put bluntly, if you were going to design a TV programme, you wouldn't choose engines* who can only go forward, backward, fast, slow and crash. (Even Bob the Builder moves around.)

You have to use age-appropriate language, so for example, you can't say, 'The Fat Controller† held a concert,' because holding's what you do to Teddy bears and ice creams. So you try a synonym. 'The Fat Controller put on a concert.' Nope that's as bad, until you get to 'It was the day of the big concert. The Fat Controller was in charge.' Just as important was guarding against inadvertent train filth such as 'Thomas pulled his load all over the Island' or 'Percy huffed and puffed but he just couldn't come'. At that time we were still operating under the dictum from *Thomas*' creator, the Reverend Wilbert Awdry, that all the steam engines were boys save for a narrow-gauge steamie called Rusty who, I was told, was sexually indeterminate and couldn't be referred to as either he or she, but only as 'Rusty' (or Betty-both-ways as he/she came to be

---

* And it's engines, never trains.
† In America you can't say 'Fat' on children's TV, so he's always Sir Topham Hatt (inherited privilege, on the other hand, is fine).

known). Awdry insisted that all female engines were diesels, thus allowing exclamations like 'Mavis was the happiest diesel on the Island!' and 'Mavis was proud of being a big diesel', which I enjoyed enormously.

You also needed to understand how a steam railway works. I now know more about trains than is either useful or attractive (Main line? Narrow gauge? Go on, ask me) and I now have a working map of the Island of Sodor in my head. (Brendham Docks, Maithwaite Station, Gordon's Hill, etc. etc.)

I took very quickly to the world of *Thomas*. It taught me to be simple again, and reminded me that it's never about what happens, it's how the characters *feel* about what happens. Train crashes and avalanches can occur, but they're not the story, the story is how the engine feels about it – do they feel left out, or act selfishly, or have to ask for help? I particularly liked the modified emotions. No one in *Thomas* gets irate or furious, or plots revenge. They get 'cross', or if pushed 'very cross'. No one's traumatized. They're 'sad' or occasionally 'upset'. *Thomas* has proven exceedingly popular with children suffering from autism because the emotions are simple, reflected in the faces and stated by the narrator clearly. 'Percy *was* delighted' (big grin). Philosophically I liked the underlying principle that you don't throw things away just because they're old or broken, you fix them and use them again. Most importantly, all squabbles have to be sorted and apologies made by teatime. Unlike real life, *Thomas* is beautifully organized and guarantees a happy ending.

Noticeboard aside, it was lovingly made. The model work was mainly done by women, who'd spend hours crafting trees, hillsides, animals by hand. Each engine had its own cabinet with sliding shelves containing dozens of handmade faces with different expressions – sniffy, happy, cold, cross – laid out on foam rubber to be attached as required. The engines were handmade (based upon real engines), and the sound stages were basically huge train sets, surrounded by men twiddling remote controls; one to go back and forth, one for the eyes and one for the steam (actually hydrochloric acid). A simple shot including five engines would still require fifteen operators, not including the director.

Meetings were still difficult. I once walked out muttering the words, 'Percy wouldn't say that!' when told to make him sarcastic. Character is plot and if you take that away for expediency's sake you're doomed. The engines are the audience.* Percy, the youngest (age two and a half), is sweet and innocent, James, the red engine, is the flash one (about three); Thomas, same age as James, is everyone's friend,† Gordon is older and pompous (possibly four), Henry the same age as Gordon, but sensitive and needing special coal, Toby and Edward are older and frailer (like Grandpa). Kids start with Percy, move on to Gordon, and then we lose them to superhero cartoons and the WWF.

---

* And it is more boys than girls, 70 per cent v. 30 per cent.
† Incidentally, this makes him the most difficult one to write for.

I've worked with some famous people in my time, but none with the international star power of *Thomas*. American actors filming elsewhere at the studios would beg to bring their kids over to the *Thomas* set. As long as they kept still while the cameras were running, and stayed out of the workshop, they were fine. (Meg Ryan's son got in and saw a model of Percy with his face off and his insides hanging out, and was near cataplectic. 'They've killed Percy! They've killed Percy!' He had to be rushed to a sound stage and shown another Percy – 'Look, he's fine.' He wasn't convinced.)

One morning security seemed tight, with men wandering around with mobile phones and guards appearing from nowhere. I asked our production manager. 'Is the President coming, or what?' 'Close,' he said. 'Posh Spice.'

Lo and behold a limo rolled up and three small boys shot out followed by Posh and her best friend from childhood. Brooklyn was a bonkers *Thomas* fan and Posh had wangled an invite, and I have to say, disruption aside, she was disappointingly lovely. She chatted to everybody, was polite and grateful, and knew to stand still and shut up when the cameras were rolling. A very normal and conspicuously good mum. (Years later when we were sharing offices with the *Guinness Book of World Records* in Euston, Michael Jackson was due to pick up some platinum disc. Security was insane, bordering on fascist. 'You're not allowed to leave,' said a bouncer muttering into his radio and barring my exit. I waited one hour . . . then two then two and half before realizing, 'Hang on! I'm a freelancer, you can't keep me here,' and left. Jackson turned up looking frail and four hours late. Everyone noted that when the Queen came down for some export award she was dead on time, and in and out of the building in twenty minutes. Classy.)

Shepperton, like any film studio, has its surreal moments. You genuinely don't know who you're going to bump into and one summer's day, on turning a corner, I was suddenly surrounded by a flock of children in Hogwarts school uniform, including three who looked like Harry, Hermione and Ron only a bit off, like in a bad dream. Turns out they were their doubles, *Harry Potter and the Chamber of Secrets'* second unit had started filming on the biggest soundstage complete with Quidditch stands, castle turrets, the flying Ford Anglia and a dirty great sign, 'WARNER BROTHERS – STRICTLY NO ENTRY', which sounded like a challenge to me. Along with fellow writer Paul* and a cunning disguise – a clipboard and bunch of keys – we wandered around quite cheerfully, and coming across the crew having lunch, swiped a few sandwiches† and chatted away. We stayed to watch them film the scene where Harry is alone on the mountaintop feeling grim and Hedwig, his snowy owl, turns up. The owl lost a couple of feathers over the dozen takes, and I asked his handler/wrangler if could I have one. 'OK, but not a tail feather,' he said, and gave

---

* Without whom the series would never have been completed.
† American catering rocks.

me a fluffy one from a wing. 'Tail feathers,' he said, 'are special.' Whether he meant mystically or financially I have no idea, but I gave it to a friend's Cub who was a huge Potter fan, and it bought me a cheap popularity, as did my largesse with *Thomas* merchandise handed out elsewhere.

Over the next three years I wrote well over sixty episodes* and changed gradually but considerably. My confidence picked up and I began to feel more solid. I liked having money, the freedom to go on holiday, buy food I liked not food I could afford. Nicer clothes, decent haircuts. A DVD player, that sort of thing, but it was paying my first tax bill that made me proud.

I didn't go mad with cash because I had other uses for it. While writing *Thomas*, I discovered, much to my surprise, that I did enjoy writing (who knew). Saving scrupulously, I turned down a full-time job with HiT (Henson International Television) when they bought *Thomas*, because I wanted to write something for myself. I resigned as script editor (but stayed on as a writer) and spent six months of the year on a screenplay – the first thing I'd written in nearly a decade that was over ten minutes long – which took six drafts and two years to finish. It got me a wonderful new agent and a clutch of interesting meetings. I was beginning to pop up on people's radar. Now was the time for me to follow through with my next idea.

---

* To be honest I've lost count, especially if you count storylining and rewrites.

I'd even developed something of a sex life. Casual, and deeply non-committal, and yes one was an actor, but for the first time since the attack I was enjoying sex, with nice men whom I liked, and nobody was getting at me. The future looked good. My heart was happy and I had enough money to live on for a year. I didn't know I'd need it.

Chapter Seventeen

If a thing's worth doing, it's worth doing badly

G. K. CHESTERTON

April 2005. Twelve years after the offence . . .

I WAS WRITING when I heard a knock at my door. Our
block has an intercom so I assumed it was Louis, but
instead found two strangers on the balcony. 'My name's
DC Andy Lawrence and I'm with the Cold Case Squad,'
said a man in his late thirties, as if he'd walked straight
off the TV. 'I'm DC Donna Mitchell from the Sapphire
Unit,' said a younger woman with dark hair and an
impossibly kind face. She asked me if I was the same
woman who was attacked at—in 1993. I told them I was.
'Have you ever heard of a Greig Strachan?' I told them
the only Strachan I'd ever heard of was Gordon. 'Can you
think of any reason why Greig Strachan's fingerprints
would be in your flat?' No. I'd never heard of him. 'Then
I think we've got him,' said DC Lawrence firmly. The
machine was back and I invited them in.

Over tea and Kit-Kats, Andy and Donna (as they were
to become) said the government had set up the Sapphire

Unit to help boost the lamentable number of rape convictions (they didn't use the word lamentable). All unsolved stranger assaults were being re-opened. There had been a change in the number of points of comparison needed to make a fingerprint match (it had been a sixteen-matching-point standard but was now twelve or fourteen), and having looked at the evidence from my case with new eyes they'd found a fingerprint match. 'Where was the print?' I asked. 'We can't tell you,' they replied (a phrase I was to become familiar with). Did I want to go ahead with the case? If not, they'd go away and that was that.

I'd been appalled by the statistics too. Over the last decade I'd noticed that news reports would sporadically report that the percentage was dropping, sometimes annually. In 1985, one in four of men accused of rape were convicted. By 2003, that had fallen to one in twenty. That's five per cent. Any lower and they might as well give every woman a gun and make it legal. Part of the increase was due to more women reporting rape, but that didn't explain the lack of prosecutions.

But I was settled in my new life, I had a great new agent, lovely safe flat, money in the bank. I was branching out and felt the right side of cheerful. I was drawing in enough money from *Thomas*, and couldn't wait to get out there and meet new people.

Part of me thought the police's arrival might be the last piece of the past I needed to tie up before reclaiming a place at the creative table. I wasn't told what the process might involve, only that they'd understand if I wasn't up to it emotionally – several of the women they'd contacted had said no, because they'd since married, had families and not told anyone. It was a secret.

The implication was that although it might be upsetting, it would be relatively straightforward. Fingerprints in my flat, huh? Sounded open and shut. Time to buck the trend I thought, and said, 'Sure – let's do it.' Donna, now my official Victim Support Officer, made a date to return to collect more statements, and within twenty minutes they were gone. But here was a chance to buck the trend.

I went back to the *Thomas* script I was working on (he had a circus to deliver), and later called my friends. We all agreed it sounded terribly exciting. As it turns out we were all wrong.

Donna came and took my 'impact statement' and I was ill-prepared for how depressing it was. What had I lost – what had I not done? Living life forward is what most of us do most of the time.

Looking backwards I saw my recent achievements melt away like butter on a hot plate. I felt single and childless in a way I hadn't before. *Thomas* wasn't such a prize – I should've been writing other things. Even my flat felt small and poky. I was doing OK, but I wasn't what you could call a success. Reacting to Donna's questions about relationships, my mental health and my work reminded me what a bloody slog it had been. It was like a chat show where they only ask about your failures and missed opportunities. Summing up the impact – lost a career, didn't have a family, childbearing years taken away from me and financially ruined – was utterly immiserating. I hated the statement so much that it's the only piece of paperwork to do with this I've never wanted to read again, not even out of curiosity.*

Unlike a lot of people whose lives take a turn for the worse, I knew whose fault it was. Time had turned him into a phantom, destructive but faceless. Now he was real and I badgered Donna for information. Who was he? Where was he from? If the police had a print match he must be in the system – what for? 'I can't tell you,' said Donna, often adding, 'even I don't know that.' I knew she was lying, and she knew I knew she was lying. But I also knew she wouldn't tell me no matter what. This creates a tension, but also underlines a truth: the police are not your friends – they're servants of the state, and only by extension of us.

I took comfort in the police's awe-inspiring pedantry. No fact was too small to be cross-checked, no statement left untaken. To give them access to my medical records, I had to sign permission slips for each person they wanted to contact, then that person had to countersign saying their comments could be used. That's every

---

* The police, however, were very positive, and later asked whether it could be used (with my name taken off) as an example of how to write an impact statement. Fools.

doctor, every social worker, every housing officer, every psychiatrist . . .

And that's twelve years after the event. They had to find them first.

It soon became apparent the case wasn't straightforward. But I wasn't told why. It was definitely his fingerprint – Donna could tell me that openly: an expert had testified, and the defence concurred. There can be controversy around fingerprints, because, unlike DNA, it's not an exact science, it's an interpretative one. Two people looking at the same fingerprint can draw two different conclusions based upon similarities and differences involved. Hence the experts come into play.

The defence didn't try to argue that it wasn't his fingerprint, but (and this was a big but) you can't date fingerprints. You can prove they were left, but not when.

Donna told me of another case she was working on where a man with previous convictions for sexual assault, whose fingerprints were found on a beer bottle in a rape victim's flat, claimed they were there because he must have touched it in the off licence. He'd never met this woman let alone had sex with her.

'Then why was your semen found in her vagina?' he was asked.

He denied it to the extent of hiring a private forensic scientist to retest the semen sample. Only when his scientist confirmed it was his semen did he plead guilty – for which he still got a third off his sentence.

I even had to sign a separate statement declaring I'd

shut the front door before running up to Peri's, so he couldn't claim to have slipped in in the fifteen minutes between the attack and the police arriving.

In conversations with Donna I remembered I'd been burgled a year before the attack. A thief had kicked the door in, grabbed a mate's toolbox and scarpered. I knew the thief hadn't been in my bedroom because we'd put on a breast-cancer benefit at a small venue I ran, and I still had over £300 cash (plus cheques) sitting on the dresser waiting to be banked, and it was still there. Plus my computer was untouched (it was a Mac in the days when Macs were rare) and my jewellery box unopened.

I had to write several statements for that one.

I kept wondering where the fingerprint was. If it was in my bedroom he was definitely guilty. But Donna's answer was always the same. 'I'm sorry, I can't tell you that.'

As a victim you're in the paradoxical position of being at the centre of everything, while being told nothing about it. 'We're not allowed to coach witnesses,' they repeat, but it's more than that. Our system is built on catching the victim unaware, making their testimony seem 'more honest' to a jury. Because it's not you versus him, it's the Crown versus him, you're a witness, a legal veal calf to be led blinkingly into the witness box when your time is called. Then you're on your own.

All the original police officers were traced (one was in Canada). They even found the officer who'd transported the forensic evidence to the police station. So punctilious is the evidence-gathering that he had to sign an additional statement saying he hadn't stopped to buy anything like cigarettes on the way.

Then one wet morning, two and a bit months later, I was at home working when Donna phoned sounding pleased. 'We've arrested him – he's been remanded into custody.'

I was stunned, and felt the need to celebrate, but as it was eleven thirty and too early for a drink I went to the fridge, and there at the back lurked a luridly pink pot of M&S raspberry jelly with bits in it. Even though it was a cold miserable day, I grabbed a spoon, put on my coat, shut the door, stood on the balcony and ate it.

Because I could go outside and he couldn't.

What was described to me as 'the legal business' started in the late autumn, and the Crown Prosecution Service found there was a case to answer. Strachan was given the opportunity to plead guilty (sparing me a trial, and getting a third off his sentence), but didn't. He didn't deny it was his fingerprint in my flat, but denied it was him who attacked me. The legal arguments rumbled on until Christmas. I was told that I wasn't allowed to know what they were about but that I shouldn't worry. Whether this not being allowed is true or not I couldn't say.

The legal system could teach the mills of God a thing or two about grinding slowly, and it wasn't until the New Year that Donna phoned to say we had a trial date – 6 February, 10.00 a.m., scheduled to run for four days.

At last, I could take my life off hold. I phoned all my friends, who were jubilantly excited, and began to prepare. In January, Donna, in accordance with new police procedures, took me to Snaresbrook Crown Court for a 'court visit'. When I was at school, it was said that all you'd find in an English court was 'maddies, baddies, saddies and Paddies'. Now things had moved on, and in an attempt to make life less awful for witnesses, the police were bound to take them to court. This is supposed to demystify the process for victims, and make taking the stand less intimidating. I'd already opted to give evidence from behind a screen* but was still curious to know how it all worked and more importantly where I would be sitting in relation to 'him'. Plus, I was just plain curious.

Snaresbrook, as it turns out, was never intended to be a court. It was built in 1843 as an infant orphan asylum to, ironically, 'provide help and protection for middle-class fatherless children without adequate means of support'. A vast Gothic complex, with gates, grounds and a lake, it possesses all the cheeriness and welcome of any other Victorian building with the word 'asylum' in the title.† Turned into a grammar school after the war, its almost natural progression into the punishment business happened in the late forties when the Home Office co-opted

---

* Your choices are screened, unscreened and video link. I was tempted by the latter, but Donna and Andy said I'd make a good live witness, and hinted I wouldn't come across as well via video.

† Designed by Sir Gilbert Scott, designer of the Albert Memorial and the Midlands Hotel at King's Cross St Pancras. You get the picture.

it into the bar. It was now, I was reliably informed, Europe's busiest court, handling over seven thousand cases a year – mine included.

Donna and I passed the main body of the complex (complete with turrets) and slipped in past security through a side entrance. Corridors that had once bustled with fatherless children now heaved with barristers darting to and fro, their mobile phones and laptops jarring anachronistically with their white wigs and black robes.

The occasional passing police officer nodded to Donna, and a court officer told us court three had broken for lunch. We entered a room that was much smaller and less dramatic than I expected. The ceiling was lower, the sound muffled by carpets, and Donna watched as I wandered from place to place, occasionally asking questions as I tried to work out where the prosecuting and defence counsels, the jury, me and Strachan would variously be sitting. ('Can I sit in the judge's chair?' 'No.') Evelyn Waugh wrote in *Decline and Fall* that anyone who'd been to an English public school would feel perfectly at home in an English prison. Well, anyone who's been to an English comprehensive will feel perfectly at home in an English court, at least physically. There's no upstairs gallery and the dock isn't raised and jutting out. It's 1980s modern, with everything on the same level, the room partitioned by fixed furniture made from municipally thick pine, and lumpen chairs covered in the same 'hard-wearing' fabric you find on public transport. Where functional meets ugly.

But at least I knew where all the main players would be on the day, including me.

I had a fortnight to kill before the start. Everyone I knew was rooting for me, and having waited for this for twelve years, I felt ready.

But to my dismay the trial date was summarily cancelled the week before, and another put in its place. As the new trial date approached, I again got myself ready, told my friends, tried to get some sleep and above all, concentrated on not wigging out. It would be over soon.

That trial date was cancelled too. Another was put in its place.

Again I prepared myself again, repeating the calls, and fielding well-wishers.

That date was cancelled. As was the next. And the next.

We were now into March, which meant I hadn't been able to work properly for over two months. It should've been over by now, and I realized the worst thing about going to trial is actually getting there. Continually being told 'It's tomorrow', then tomorrow being told 'It's Friday' and Friday being told 'It's next week' is unbearable. It almost became embarrassing having to field concerned calls from friends. 'No, it hasn't happened. No, I don't know when it's going to be, they can't tell me. Yes, I'll let you know . . .'

My life was spent waiting for 'lists' to be put up, which the barristers relay to the police, who then relay it to me. I've never been very good at waiting. I'll walk rather than wait for a bus, and leave a shop if there are more than three people in a queue. Knowing every day that the call could come for tomorrow (you were only guaranteed twenty-four hours' notice) meant working became impossible, sleep a luxury and the temptation to quit almost irresistible.

Three weeks into March a trial date held. On a cold grey morning Donna collected me and friends Marsha and Amanda and drove us to Snaresbrook, where we were led in through the back.

Seated in the witness waiting area (along with other witnesses in other trials), I was presented with the floor plans of my old flat. At last, I discovered what Donna and the others had known all along. There, marked with a red cross, was the spot where his fingerprint was found. On the *inside* of my bedroom door. I was then shown the police photos that had been taken that morning at Peri's, which were to be presented to the jury. Looking at a younger you is always strange, a younger battered you doubly so. I was less upset than curious: was that really me? And didn't long hair suit me? As I was taking it all in, my inappropriate vanity was interrupted by a middle-aged woman plonking herself next to me, smelling so strongly of heavy perfume and cigarettes that she reminded me of the Seventies. She was 'our' barrister. She told me she couldn't discuss the case with me, then patted me on the shoulder, said I'd be fine and vanished. That was as far as the conversation went.

A court official appeared and led Amanda and Marsha to the public gallery (really just six seats at the back) but I had to wait while they removed Strachan from court.

I took my place in the witness box, looked at the court and the court looked at me. The jury were opposite, the judge to my left and a large brown baffle board to my right. Then Strachan was led back in and I found it strangely gratifying to hear the clanking of the warden's keys.

As I sat down after taking my oath (no God) my head started to swim and I asked the judge if I could have some water. A clerk swiftly appeared with a cup and those were the last few seconds when I felt I had a say in the proceedings.

As 'our' barrister opened with questions about the night of the attack, I was aware of the jury as a mass, not individuals. It was only when describing Strachan physically I noticed their eyes flicking to the other side of the board and I wondered if what I was saying matched what they could see. I was asked about my cleaning habits, and having been a chambermaid said I was good at cleaning, and did it regularly. It was all over in about twenty-five minutes.

It was the defence's turn and his barrister stood. A Home Counties woman, sixty-ish, blonde hair, heavy-jowled and baby pink lipstick which was a mistake.

She started in a 'sincere voice', a judicial echo of 'soft voice tilty head' that had followed me around for years, and announced the defence was *of course* not disputing I'd been attacked and I found myself saying, 'Thank you,' which annoyed me. I realized Donna's advice to 'just tell the truth', although comforting in the abstract, provided no clues as to the rules of engagement. Was I allowed to say, 'Well, that's big of you'?

'I see you kept your wallet in the kitchen,' she started.

I immediately said yes, which was true and it wasn't. I'd dropped it next to the kettle on the night of the attack because I was desperate for a cup of tea, but I didn't 'keep' it there as a matter of course. But saying yes allowed her to launch into questions about pizza-delivery men. In the six years I'd lived in that flat, did I ever ask pizza-delivery men into the kitchen to pay them? ('No.') Did I ever ask them to bring the pizza through because my hands were full? ('No.') When she asked me whether I'd ever asked a man to bring the pizza in because the box was 'too hot' and finally 'too heavy' I didn't know whether I was allowed to say 'Are you insane?' or 'Don't you eat pizza in Esher?'

I'd twigged she was trying to place this man in my bedroom consensually, but didn't know how long was I expected to answer dumb questions without reacting to their idiocy (about an hour as it turned out).

After similarly tortuous questions about gasmen, electricity men, postmen (did you ever have a package that was so heavy you etc. . .), she started in on men in local pubs, making the fact that I *had* drunk in local pubs sound like an admission.

Did I ever talk to men in pubs? (I've no idea, I must

have.) 'Surely in all your conversations with men in pubs, you must have had one so fascinating you said, "Let's finish this at my place?"' ('No.') 'What, really?' ('No.') 'Never?' ('No.') 'Are you telling the court that in all your years of *drinking* in pubs you never once had a conversation so *fascinating* you felt the need to finish it later?' ('No.') 'So you've never been out with friends and . . . etc. . . .' into endless variations of 'did you pick men up at pubs', all in a tone of scepticism, implying I was withholding something from the court. ('Oh, you're right, I forgot – I *was* a slut.')

Did I ever have workmen in? (A friend was a builder.) Painters and decorators? (My next-door neighbour Martin.) Finally she hit on motorcycle couriers. I must have used them *and* asked them into my bedroom as that's where my computer was. I said no I didn't use couriers, and even if I did I wouldn't ask one into my bedroom.

Her eyebrows shot up in disbelief. 'Really?' Still shaking her head, she continued, 'Are you sure there wasn't one draft that absolutely had to be there *that* afternoon because etc., etc. . . .'

I finally explained I'd worked on sketch shows that were time-contingent, but the musical was a major piece that took three years to complete.

She turned to the jury with a knowing smile. 'Oh, I'm sure we'd all like three years to finish something.'

I was dumbstruck. Implying I'd fucked the Household Cavalry might be germane to the defence but sneering at me? If there was one thing I'd been foolishly certain about, it was that, having been attacked in my own bed, in my own flat, in the middle of the night, I would be spared personal attack. Maybe I should count myself lucky she didn't ask me how much I'd been drinking or what I'd been wearing to bed. But yet again, she knew the rules of engagement, I didn't. Before I could point out that I'd have liked to get to thirty without being attacked, she'd moved on to my flatmate's sexual history, asking whether I knew her 'male acquaintances', and any other men she might have 'brought home' as if that were a regular thing. Still simmering, I gathered myself and said we'd been at the same comprehensive so yes, I did know her 'male acquaintances' and her boyfriend – singular.

Her last personal dig was during questions about the burglary. I explained (again) the burglar had simply grabbed the tools and left, and I knew they hadn't gone into my bedroom because the breast-cancer-benefit cash was still there, as was my computer (a Mac, both portable and desirable as stolen goods go).

She asked whether having reported the incident to the police I later pursued it. I said no, it wasn't that serious a crime.

'Well, maybe not to you,' she replied. 'After all, they weren't *your* tools that were stolen.'

I wasn't taking that. I told her *I'd* paid for my friend's tools to be replaced, and was sure that if asked he would agree that having a toolbox stolen was slightly less serious than being attacked by a rapist. Now fuck off and take your ugly pills.

I was eventually released from the court. Donna said I'd done well, my friends said they were proud and I was furious but relieved.

'Thank God that's over,' I said. If only.

The next afternoon I was surprised to find Donna at my door. By then I'd succumbed to the flu, but aware money was thin on the ground, had taken on some work for the *Daily Telegraph*, and was forcing myself to write. Bleary-eyed and wearing pyjamas, I let her in.

She looked unhappy, and I knew something was up. Earlier that day, while DC Lawrence was on the stand, the defence had introduced something 'that made Strachan look good', something they knew they weren't allowed to, but leaving the judge no option but to dismiss the jury.

There was going to be a retrial. For the first time since the whole damned thing began I burst into tears.

Chapter Eighteen

Some circumstantial evidence is very strong,
as when you find a trout in the milk.

HENRY DAVID THOREAU

MARCH LUMBERED ON, and three courses of antibiotics later I was still ill, only now I had thrush too. When I caught the sleeve of my dressing gown on the hob and poured boiling water over my hand blistering it like bubblewrap (I still have a scar) it became so absurd I slid to the floor laughing. I knew there was only one thing to do – find someone worse off than me. So I phoned my friend Russell, who had liver cancer. He wasn't allowed to visit because I was ill and he was in chemo, but he did some food shopping for me, left it at the foot of the stairs and we waved at each other from a safe distance.

The rest of the time I lay in bed tormented by what did 'made him look good' mean? Was he working with handi-capped kids? Had he repented, if so why was he pleading not guilty? Was this a bloody waste of time? If I'd heard what had been said in open court it would've been fine, but the police thought it better I be kept in the dark (again).

It was infuriating, but by now I'd spent enough time with Donna to believe she had my best interests at heart. I also knew that beneath her doe-eyed kindness lay a woman who had every episode of *The Shield* on DVD. So for want of a better plan I decided to trust her.

I had a eureka moment too when I realized the defence was operating on a misassumption – that I'd lived in the flat continually for six years. I'd missed it in court because I was busy being wrong-footed, but I'd actually moved out after four years, only moving back in after my flatmate Steph went travelling and I could have the place to myself.

More significantly, in between her going away and me moving back in, Martin painted the place brilliant white from top to bottom (it was the nineties).

So to hell with pizza-delivery men, and how often I cleaned, the print *had* to have got there after I'd moved back in. I wrote a statement, Peri and Martin wrote supporting statements, and a new trial date was set for May.

By early April I was finally back at work and enjoying it – it was so much more fun than real life. But as I was settling down, May was sneaking up.

I started mentally preparing for the legal trickery weeks before. And clothes. Last time I'd dressed like a respectable plain Jane, in a brown jumper and plain skirt. But if they were going to suggest I'd invited Strachan into my bedroom consensually (and they didn't have to prove it, just suggest 'reasonable doubt'), then I was going to say, one cashmere jumper and discreet gold earring at a time, that not only wouldn't I fuck Strachan, I wouldn't even mix socially with him. I didn't care if that made me a snob. I'd have dressed in a harlequin outfit if I'd thought it would help.

I was feeling positive until the next three trial dates were cancelled one after another, each cancellation accompanied by the same 'This is it . . . finally, this is *it*' followed by the calamitous let-down. My lack of influence on the process was maddening. Four months after the supposed start date, we were barely at the beginning. Film meetings came and I struggled through them – feeling the opportunities slipping away.

Nothing I said, felt, or wanted was even acknowledged by the legal process. Instead, everything I had grafted for over the previous years, financially and emotionally, was being dismantled, one cancellation at a time. I'd completed *one* piece of work in four months, and couldn't take on any more until I knew when this bloody process would be over, yet I was expected to be ready at the process's whim.

'I can't afford this,' I told Donna, 'it's killing me.'

I was furious to be worrying about money again. Self-employed people don't get holiday or sick pay, they have to find work, do the work and schedule it in. I genuinely don't believe I'm greedy – I've never fantasized about possessions. I've known rich people and poor people, and noticed those with twenty-three million pounds in the bank weren't twenty-three times happier that those with one million, and I have known poor people who were content. Happiest of all, though, were those in the middle – where I'd managed to get to.

'Why don't you sign on?' said a well-meaning friend, and I was tempted.

During the five days spent waiting for the next trial date (also cancelled) I became despondent. I was desperately unhappy, incredulous that Strachan, with the connivance of the law, was doing me over again. The only two fuckers in that courtroom not getting paid were him and me, and he was getting free meals.

Instead of RoboCop, I lapsed into Lady Vengeance.* But only when I had the energy. Rage is not a fun companion, and playing Fantasy Fatwah was exhausting, and coupled with a lack of sleep and a moving finishing line I worried that I was going mad, and I fell into an awful slump. It was impossible to escape the conclusion that I'd been better off before the police arrived. So far I had gained nothing, lost hugely and knew I had worse to come.

In case you have any doubts, taking the stand is a horrible experience. I'm a sturdy literate woman, and I found it intimidating. How somebody who's been recently attacked could bear it is beyond me. Most people don't like personal conflict, we go out of our way to avoid it,

---

* Korean thriller directed by Chan-Wook Park, about a young woman who exacts revenge on a child-killer, inviting the children's parents to participate.

particularly in Britain, where the correct response to being jabbed in the eye with an umbrella or having our toes stepped on is to say sorry.

If you've ever bought a piece of AV equipment and received a letter from the TV Licensing authority assuming you're a cheat and threatening you (despite the fact that if they checked they'd see you had a licence) then you'll have some idea of a barrister's tone.

It's accusatory, and entering the witness box means putting yourself in a position where highly educated and experienced people are paid to twist your words, trip you up and quite possibly sneer at you, because if their client's innocent, then *you* must be lying, and therefore it is appropriate for them to regard you with derision. They do this every day of their working lives, and excel at moral superiority, mock outrage and feigned incredulity ('Are you seriously trying to tell the court . . .'), the dull catechisms of their trade. The extraordinary paradox at the heart of our justice system is that the people who are most disadvantaged in a court are those who've never been in trouble.

I asked DC Lawrence if he liked giving evidence. 'Oh no, I hate it,' he said, 'I always get nervous, all policemen do.' And they know what to expect.

This was not the perfect lead-in to taking the stand and I was so ragged, on more than one occasion I seriously contemplated giving up, but more often wished it would all go away.

*

I needed to decide. That sounds a bit George Bush-like ('I'm the decider') but if I was going to continue, then I needed to stop focusing on the unfairness and whining and find a reason to carry on. I took stock and accepted that, OK I was taking a hammering, but I had a council flat, my rent was low and they'd have a hell of a time throwing me out. Second, there's always more work. Third, a strong anachronistic sense of duty* kicked in. He was a bad man and needed to go to prison. The wicked mustn't be allowed to get away with it because of the passage of time. Whenever I'd seen news stories about Nazi-hunters dragging some decrepit seventy-year-old mass-murderer through court, I always thought, 'Good – at least you didn't die in bed.'

A friend, Christine, came over from the Isle of Man to baby-sit me, and after another sleepless night, I knew what I wanted to do. I wanted to see Rembrandt. One of the wonderful quirks of London is that you can be living on a seventies concrete council estate, and at the same time be ten minutes away from one of the finest paintings in the world.†

She drove me to Kenwood House and I stood in front of his self-portrait as an older man. It always astonishes me that a man would want to memorialize his relative failure and do it so magnificently. Most classical portraits bore me

---

* Thanks, Mum.
† *Self-Portrait* by Rembrandt (1661),
http://en.wikipedia.org/wiki/Kenwood_House.

because they're of rich people surrounded by their status symbols – wife, children, spaniels, manservant, etc. They're dull no matter how good the lace is. Rembrandt is surrounded by earth brown and gold space, like he wants to draw attention to the things he lacks. He's not wealthy and successful, it's just him, melancholy and defiant – with a paintbrush and palette. Only the clothes and garb date it. Like all oil paintings, it changes depending on where you stand. Watched closely by a guard (very closely) I inched forward, until the canvas was fluffs and spots of colour, brushstrokes that made no sense but proved this was the work of a human hand. And then just as slowly I drew back and the picture took shape and the man appeared. It was like staring up at the night sky. Not in London where there's light pollution but in the country where it's Bible-black, but full of stars. It gave me a sense of scale.

You . . . are . . . *here*.

Twenty minutes and a bacon sandwich later I was much refreshed. I slept relatively well that night and was delighted when next morning the trial date held. Donna collected me, Christine and another friend Garry and drove us to Snaresbrook through the Friday traffic. By now I was not one of the innocents. I knew the drill. I was introduced to our new barrister, shown my statement, then Donna and my friends were led into court.

The clerk returned for me. Strachan was led out, I was led in. We had a new male judge, puffy, round-faced, with a hint of colour in his cheeks, like a judge from central casting. While standing to take the oath I noticed two women in the public gallery that I took to be members of Strachan's family. Not the cashmere type.

Our barrister started and told the court I was a playwright. I corrected her, I *used* to be a playwright, but hadn't worked for eight years after the attack and now wrote *Thomas Tank* and for the *Daily Telegraph* (one of the few occasions those have ever worked as a name-drop). She asked me about the night and I again described my attacker; white, medium build (about the same height and weight as an ex-boyfriend), rough angular face and thin lips. A few more questions and our side was done.

Strachan had a new barrister. There in Muttley's place stood an ageing posh white man with droopy eyes and deceptively sympathetic face. He said of course the defence wasn't questioning I'd been attacked and being reflexively polite I again said thank you.

I'd been told about the new judge and Strachan's new barrister. It never occurred to me he might have a completely new defence. We were returning to a familiar theme of yesteryear. Black guy, was it?

Droopy started with the sophistry. 'I see that according to your statement you were stopped in the street by a black man?' (With emphasis on *blaaaack maan*.)

Just as drinking in pubs had a subtext in the first trial, so an implied danger was to be read into the presence of a black male on the street in the small hours. So the 'boy' became a man, and the friendly approach a threat.

I said he didn't 'stop me', he asked for a fag and I liked him, which is why I gave him two.

'But from where *he* was standing he could see the front door to your flat?'

I said he wasn't looking at the door, he was looking at the cigarettes.

'But looking over your shoulder *he* could see your front door?'

Yet again I found myself defending a young man I'd met only fleetingly. But it mattered to me. He was the last contact with my old life, and to have him associated with another man's violence seemed terribly wrong. I insisted he *wasn't* looking at the door, and was asked to pick up the board in my witness pack with the blown-up photos of my old street and point to where we were standing. I did so.

'So . . . *he* could see your front door, then?'

I denied it, and Droopy continued. 'Maybe he doubled back or sneaked around the block?' I pointed at the boards. 'No. No. He went *that* way.' Eventually Droopy ended the black man questions, but in a manner suggesting the matter was still open.

And then on to the attempted rape. In the first trial Muttley had avoided really grisly questions but Droopy had no such qualms. How many times, he asked, did my attacker stick his tongue into my mouth? And how deep? Did I bite him hard?

I said yes, and mimed biting, involuntarily saying 'fucker' (as in 'take that, fucker'). Christine snorted behind me, and the ticker-tape man committed it to court record.

He said if I bit him *that* hard there must've been blood,

and asked me where it went. I said, bluntly, 'Probably down my throat, which is why I needed an AIDS test.' He drew my attention to a line in my statement and asked me what I meant.

I had blood on the right side of my face. I do not think it was mine.

I said it meant when the statement was taken I didn't think it was my blood, but I'm not a forensic expert so I couldn't say.

He wouldn't let it go. How much blood was there? Was I sure it *all* went down my throat? Wasn't it possible the blood on my face was his?

Even at the time I thought it was a good thing I'm not very sensitive. I repeated I wasn't a forensic expert, but thought it highly likely the blood on my face was my blood (I was tempted to add I was sure the blood on the walls was mine too but didn't).

'Then why did you say at the time you didn't think it was yours?'

I said at the time I didn't know my nose was broken in two places and would need extensive surgery. I irritatedly mimed wiping my nose to demonstrate how easy it would've been to spread my blood across my face unwittingly. For the first time I noticed the jury and they were wincing.

Droopy tried a new tack. A police officer had written into his notes I'd said my attacker had a cockney accent and pressured me to admit I'd said this. I shrugged and said I had no idea. I told him I didn't remember his accent or telling anyone he was a cockney.

Surely, he said, as a writer I must be 'good at accents'?

I asked what 'good at accents' meant. Did he mean I was good at doing them? and we went round and round until I pointed out the rapist was saying, 'Shut the fuck up, you bitch, or I'll kill you,' whilst punching me in the face. It *wasn't* a conversation. At no point did I go, 'Oh! Is that a hint of Geordie?'

He continued. 'On the night of the accident . . .' I waited for him to catch himself and glanced at the judge but he was busy writing something down. I leant into the mike and cut across. 'It *wasn't* an accident,' I pointed out firmly.

'I didn't say accident, I said "incident",' he replied sharply. In the only comic moment of the proceedings, a murmur of 'Oh no you didn't' crept rhubarb-style around the court, and the judge looked up.

Droopy made a weak joke ('Age don't you know, ha ha') and then apologized, first to the judge, then to the court and finally to me. Of course he didn't mean 'accident' of course of *course*. I just smiled. Yeah, *now* you're being sensitive.

Finally, after having testified for over ninety minutes that I'd been attacked by a white man, Droopy closed with the defence's final question.

'Are you *sure* it wasn't a black man?'

An old Paul Merton joke flashed into my mind. 'I

dunno, I only saw his face – they're very clever these black men', but I said, no, absolutely not, 100 per cent certain. He was white, definitely *definitely* not a black man, no.

I was released from court.

I spent the evening phoning friends, then had one of those weekends when everybody thinks someone else is looking after you and leaves you alone. It was lovely. Feeling the need for a distraction I reached for an old friend from childhood, *The Code of the Woosters* (the one where Gussie hands out the school prizes), and as with all my favourite books I sat down and read it as slowly as possible.

Bertie did the business, and on Monday my friend Reg came over with a baseball documentary about Jackie Robinson. As we were watching, Donna phoned. The prosecution had finished and I could now be told what the jury knew, and what the police had known from the start.

Strachan was a convicted rapist. He'd broken in and raped a woman in her corridor. He'd only been out of prison for seven months when he attacked me. The jury could be told of his conviction because of new 'bad character' legislation (this was the cause of all the legal arguments). As for 'made him look good', it was nothing to do with sick kiddies or acts of charity. No, in the world of the criminal scumbag claiming you're 'just a burglar' qualifies as looking good. Muttley had made a police officer reveal on the stand that Strachan had been convicted of three burglaries in Scotland, but this had already been ruled inadmissible because he'd also indecently assaulted the women living there. Why he wasn't prosecuted for this is a mystery and I've been told everything from 'It's a different legal system' to more worryingly 'We've lost the files'. Nevertheless all three women wrote new statements, and two were prepared to come to court (the third was heavily pregnant and found the whole thing traumatic). Suggesting he was 'just a burglar' was misleading so the jury had to be dismissed.

I never thought I'd be pleased to hear someone was a rapist, but I was overjoyed – it *had* been worthwhile and he was going down. Donna doused my good cheer and counselled caution. All the defence had to do was convince three jury members of reasonable doubt and he'd walk. You never can tell.

I got off the phone and actually felt brave for the first time. I'd always been privately ashamed at losing my voice, not screaming or shouting. Now I felt I'd got it back. I hadn't liked to admit it before, not to myself or anybody, even a therapist, but part of me harboured a fear that he was in fact just a crappy rapist, and that I'd made too much of the attack. I wish I'd thought more about the first victim, but I was completely happy and relieved. Reg gave me a bear hug and we went back to Jackie Robinson's hell-life.

On Tuesday I sat at home while the defence set out their stall. Strachan had no character witnesses or alibis, only a legal-aid solicitor ('scruffy looking' according to Donna) to say he'd advised him to give a 'no comment' interview.

Strachan took the stand. So, how did his fingerprint get into my bedroom? What was his justification for putting me through all this again? A magical alibi?

He claimed he was the burglar who'd stolen the toolbox. Our barrister asked what types of tools were taken. (They were highly specialized window-fitting tools.) He said he 'couldn't remember'. Why, if he'd been in my bedroom, didn't he take the money in plain view? He said he 'must have missed it'. Lastly he was asked to give a date when he thought he'd burgled my flat. He gave a date, and it was pointed out to him he was in prison at the time.

And that was the defence's case.

After summing up ('the black guy done it'), the jury was sent out to deliberate.

On Wednesday I got up and waited. Court starts at 10 a.m., and by twelve thirty I'd heard nothing and started pacing. By one o'clock nothing and I was getting concerned when my buzzer went. It was Donna. I let her up and opened the door. 'Guilty,' she said, beaming. 'Twelve–nil.'

Thirteen years after the attack, fourteen months after the police arrived at my door, it had taken a jury of twelve men and women less than twenty minutes to unanimously find him guilty. I bounced around the flat delirious that it was over, over.

Chapter Nineteen

Hurry up and wait

US ARMY MAXIM

SENTENCING WAS SET for July, in two months' time. After the high of the verdict I returned to earth with a crash, after I discovered that witnesses get nothing for loss of earnings, and I was entitled to merely £88.50 expenses, and to claim that I had to fill in a four-page form (it didn't have a box for 'kiss my arse' so I didn't bother).

But at least I was near the finishing line. I just needed to know how long he'd get. It was important to me. Never mind measuring out your life in coffee spoons, I'd had my suffering quantified every which way and for every purpose for over a decade. Now it was the law's turn. How much was I worth?

I thought that it was all over bar the shouting, and following a dismal meeting with my accountant, tried to put the trial out of mind and pick up some work. The 2006 World Cup came and went and so did the first sentencing date (cancelled two days before). After answering the emails and calls (what did he get?) and rearranging for friends to come on the next date, I started to anticipate the final showdown.

A week later I gathered my friends for the next Big Day. People arranged days off work, others re-scheduled gigs, everyone moved things around, but that was cancelled too, again at forty-eight hours' notice. I couldn't be given a new date, the judge was going on holiday, so it would take another four weeks *just to set the new date . . .*

August passed and a new date was set, September 11th. Everyone commented on the notability of the date, but I stopped short of asking anyone if they wanted to come as I was too embarrassed. I couldn't bear the thought of another 'it's not happening' ringaround. I was right, and when September 11th was cancelled too I noticed even the police were starting to sound embarrassed.

Whether it was because the probation service failed to complete a report, or the prison service failed to release him to see a doctor, or the defence made a last-minute request for more time ceased to matter. It was the institutional equivalent of 'the dog ate my homework'.

I was tired of being upset and bored of hearing myself complain. Misery doesn't love company, it sucks the life out of it. You can't even have casual conversations with your neighbours. What's going on, how are you? is a question you want to avoid. When an Arsenal fan drove into the back of me on Hornsey Lane (he was admiring the new stadium) it genuinely made a refreshing change. This was a misfortune I could tell people about.

Finally, we had a date, 18 September, that held. Punch-drunk on anti-climax, I began to prepare myself (again) for seeing Strachan. I'd not seen or heard him since that night. He was a jangle of keys from behind the baffle board.

But now I was going to see him in the flesh. I had no idea how I'd react, or what it would mean to me. Would it change my life, or be like Mao's verdict on the French Revolution – still too soon to tell? But after eighteen months, it was going to happen. Above everything I wanted to know: what was his excuse?

Andy asked me to write a letter to the judge, describing how Strachan's refusal to plead guilty thus forcing a trial had affected me. I laid it on thick.

Dear Judge

This is just a short letter to let you know how incredibly upsetting and disruptive I've found the trial process to be. Having destroyed my life and career once, the process of bringing this man to trial has driven a coach and horses through my life again. Getting from a comprehensive school (I didn't have the opportunity to go to college) to the West End was a monumental struggle in the first place.

Now, nearly 19 months after this whole process began I find the income of my new career has halved, my savings are gone and I haven't had a holiday in two years. The stress has caused me to start smoking again, and I'm back on anti-depressants.

The most distressing consequence has been the

extreme mood swings. Trying to write (especially for children) when fighting feelings of fear, despair and impotent rage has been a nightmare. My personal relationships have suffered too. I'm not much fun to be around at times.

Although I feel grateful to live in a country where the police and state genuinely try and catch these kinds of men, I am still shocked at how painful and gruelling it's been for me as a witness. I've been tempted to give up on more than one occasion.

I have sensed no remorse or pity from this man, just a vile determination to deny the truth. He's a violent rapist who has no place in civilised society.

I sincerely hope you will send him to prison for as long as possible. Then perhaps I can get on with rebuilding my life – for the third and hopefully final time.

Yours faithfully

Amanda, my Korean American friend, said you should always have a big black man sitting next to you in court, and luckily Reg, who's American and both, said he'd come.

On the 18th, the police collected us and drove to court where we met my Australian friend Marsha and Garry from Up North. Looking like the United Colours of Benetton we filed through security (Reg was the only one stopped) and waited outside the court. Andy took my letter to the judge while 'our' latest barrister made the customary flying visit, and I became aware of how desperately I wanted this over with.

As Amanda ran down the list of things she hoped would happen to Strachan in prison, I noticed a solitary white man in his thirties, dressed smartly but looking uncomfortable, standing to one side. 'Is he coming in with us?' I muttered to Andy. Andy shrugged – anyone can go into court – and pointed out a couple of local journalists.

My party's high spirits was in stark contrast to this man's unease, and when the usher appeared and we filed into court, he entered last. Strachan was led in, and while I was eyeballing him, the two men exchanged glances. Ah, so he was a brother.

The judge came in, sat down and we were off.

From the moment Droopy opened his mouth I knew it wasn't going to happen. A report had been delivered late or something. My body felt heavy and my bones sank into the chair as I listened to Droopy's legal righteous indignation, his client couldn't possibly be sentenced like this, it wouldn't be right or fair . . . Andy, sitting with the prosecuting counsel, shook his head with disbelief, and the judge capped it all by granting the delay, saying that as I'd waited thirteen years for justice, he was sure I 'wouldn't mind waiting another twenty-eight days or so'.

In my letter I'd said the last eighteen months had seen my income halved, I was back on anti-depressants, had started smoking and hadn't had a holiday in two years.

What in the above would lead anyone to think I 'wouldn't mind'? I was staggered, and a part of me gave up.

When the call went out, 'All rise!' I found myself just sitting there. The court didn't respect me, so why should I respect the court?

Outside, Andy tried to explain the causes for the delay, but I walked off and stood in a patch of September sunlight. Blanketed by my friends' sympathy I asked to be driven home and left alone.

I went a bit mad that night, and was shocked the next morning to find I'd woken up crying. I was starting to crave oblivion and realized it was caring that was killing me. So I did my best to stop. It took another couple of days of raging and whining, but eventually I reached a comforting state of near disinterest.

When a new sentencing date was set for six weeks' time, I wasn't sure I was going to go. But to my surprise the judge asked the police to pass on an apology to me, and let it be known he was determined it should happen on the 30th. It was moved to the 31st, Halloween.

I was feeling quite low key, so I didn't ask for support en masse. Instead, Donna picked up Amanda and me and we drove past shops displaying scream masks, witches' hats and pumpkins, arriving at court with minutes to spare.

The brother was there, looking, if possible, even more embarrassed than last time. I was introduced to our latest barrister, then we were led in. The door to the dock swung open and Strachan walked in.

I was shocked. He'd put on weight, a good stone since I'd last seen him, and my body physically recoiled. It recognized the man that attacked me in a way it hadn't before. It was in his shoulders, neck and jawline. I didn't stare, and he didn't look at me once.

The judge was up to speed with the paperwork, so our barrister had little to do. Which left Droopy to make Strachan's case for mitigation – drugs and alcohol made him do it, and now he was a Catholic he was all better. Letters were produced from priests, imams and prison wardens saying what a perfect prisoner he was.

He claimed Strachan, 'saddened' about how his life was going, had 'completely reformed himself'.

I was very good and said nothing (I'd promised Andy). It was only when Droopy claimed Strachan had made 'reparation as best he can' that I went, 'Ha!' And, as Bertie would say, I meant it to sting.

Droopy argued that as Strachan had received only six years for his previous rape and two years for a sexual assault on an eleven-year-old girl (which ran concurrently), the judge couldn't possibly give him more here – especially as his attack on me was 'not as ghastly as it might be'. He also said Strachan had had 'an agony' over the trials and waiting for sentence.

There was a break while the judge thought things over, during which time our barrister showed me Strachan's letter to the judge, which was handwritten in black biro on lined prison paper. It wasn't a scrawl, it was well written. Without admitting guilt, he extended to me 'his deepest sympathies' for the 'horrific incident' and said working at the ambulance call centre (which is where he was arrested) was the best job he'd ever had. He talked about his 'faith' and what comfort he'd gathered from returning to the religion of his childhood. I felt nothing but contempt, not just for him, but for the priests, imams and wardens – none of whom withheld their support for him on the grounds that he was an unrepentant violent serial sex offender, or seemingly had any success in convincing a clearly guilty man to 'fess up and repent, sparing me this ordeal. God had forgiven him, and that made everything all right.

I discovered his address – he'd been living in the same borough, two hundred yards from friends. I'd driven past that road a hundred times. I was disgusted, as I was to find he was working for a private company, hired by the NHS, taking calls from vulnerable people. Don't these companies have to do checks of any sort? Would you want to dial 999 and speak to a serial rapist and child-sex offender?

In some ways it was better this way. I'm fairly Jacobean when it comes to law and order, but if Strachan had pleaded guilty from the off and shown true remorse I would have had to forgive him. It would have been hellishly difficult, but if he'd confessed and said sorry he would have proved he was no longer the man who attacked me. I would still have wished a prison sentence on him, but any enmity would be directed at the man he used to be, not any present incarnation. It was not to be.

'Fuck him,' I thought and handed the letter back to Andy.

The judge returned. He said my impact statement made for 'grim reading'. Despite conceding that it had not been proved that Strachan was still a danger to women, he said the 'dreadful crime' warranted a 'determined' sentence of eleven years.

There was no banging of gavels, no 'Do you have anything to say to the court?' – he just kept on talking. Strachan looked pale and I was delighted if confused. Was that it? Was that the sentence? The court was asked to rise. This time I sprang to my feet. Strachan exchanged glances with his brother before being led away.

Outside it became clear that eleven years was a terrific result. I felt tired but vindicated. Happy would be pushing it. But I was thrilled for Andy, who'd worked on the case for more than two years. 'Of course he'll appeal,' he said. 'They always do.'

Amanda had brought party poppers and we celebrated. The eager local journos came and asked me how I felt. I said I was pleased it was over. Did I think justice had been done? 'No,' I said. 'Justice would be if you tied him to a chair and gave me a tyre iron.' I caught myself and added, 'That's off the record.'

And then we went home for tea.

Andy had asked whether I'd mind if he gave my number

to magazines who periodically contacted the Sapphire Unit looking for stories. 'Sure,' I said, not knowing what to expect, but thinking maybe I could drum up publicity for the unit, which would be no bad thing.

Over the next few days a series of earnest young women from magazines like 'Take a Break' or 'Have A Coffee' called to offer me five hundred pounds for my story. 'Don't worry,' they said reassuringly, 'you won't have to write anything.' Bless. I passed.

More startling was seeing the story in the London press* under the banner 'Writer's 13 Year Rape Battle Ends' which ended with:

> Outside Snaresbrook Crown Court, the unnamed woman, 41, blew a party whistle in celebration. 'There's a huge sense that it's over,' she said. 'True justice would be if I was left to my own devices in a room with him and had a tyre iron – but 11 years is great. I'd like the law changed to introduce chemical castration.

So much for 'off the record'. This story was picked up, and ran in many papers.

Getting back to life after the trial was a drearily familiar nightmare. My income had dropped from £43,000 the year before the trial to £17,246. Take off agents' fees, and tax, and I'd have been better off on benefit. The only consolation was hearing he'd only got six years for his pre-

---

* *Metro*, 1 November 2006.

vious rape and assaulting the eleven-year-old girl. If he had, as he claimed, got himself a great new life, then I'm glad I could come in and fuck it up for him.

The physical relief was overwhelming and I ate and ate, and slept and slept, as if trying to reboot my whole system. I had a huge amount of contempt to let go of. The justice system is the only institution I've come across that makes the DSS look well run and cost-effective. If it were a company it wouldn't just go out of business, its customer base would burn it to the ground.

No matter what people said about 'it must be a relief now it's over' and 'now you can have closure' I was left with more a sense of 'Well, that happened.' It really did feel as if I'd just been dragged through an old-fashioned play – more pantomime than high drama – complete with silly costumes, unknown rules, archaic language.

Some of it just didn't make sense. I can't remember the name of any of 'our' barristers because I met them so fleetingly, and even that was rendered utterly pointless by their immediately saying, 'Of course, we can't talk about the case.' Other than that, Mrs Lincoln, what did you think of the play? What *else* is there to talk about ten minutes before you testify in a rape trial? Got any plans for the weekend? It's asinine and confusing.

The fancy dress doesn't help. Looking across a sea of wigs and up at the judge in his wig and red-and-black robes didn't make me think, 'Oh, the noble traditions of British justice,' but 'Fuck me, it's 1830 – I must get my chimney swept.' Just because something's old, doesn't make it special. Everything about an English courtroom from the 'Crown' prosecution downwards clearly sells the story that justice is something posh people dispense through powers vested in them from above, rather than it is our right as citizens to have a legal system that represents us and upholds our laws and values. Just as politicians of all political parties and footballers of whatever team have more in common with each other than they do with their supporters, so barristers have more in common with each other than with their clients. It's a different world and a different language.

It feels archaic, because of course it is. Women weren't even allowed to sit on juries until 1928. All the rules and codes of conduct were set in place long before we got there. The reason it's adversarial, rather than, say, inquisitorial, is because it's based upon old Greek and Roman male ideas of rhetoric and argument as re-invented by the Victorians. It's not fit for purpose for all sorts of crimes. Take gang crime. Its strictures on evidence allow no protective facility for witnesses, who know they'll be physically harmed if they testify. The judicial response is that if they won't show their face, then they can't testify. The end. That young people are killing each other and gang culture is destroying communities is not their problem.

Similarly the idea that 'it's better for ninety-nine guilty men to go free, than one innocent man to go to prison' is proffered as a divine truth – the 'golden thread of British justice' – rather than a relative value. I could make a very good argument that it is better societally to lock up ninety-nine child molesters at the expense of one innocent man – if only by adding up the number of victims who would be saved. (Looking at the convictions for rape, people who believe this must be deliriously happy.)

In contrast to the women in Scotland who weren't allowed their moment in court, Strachan was allowed to lie and lie and lie, at no additional cost. Criminals get a third off their sentence if they plead guilty, but nothing added on for blatant perjury. Mark Dixie, who raped and murdered Sally Anne Bowman, put forward the defence that he came across Sally Anne's prone body and 'took advantage' of the situation by having sex with her before realizing that she was dead, having not noticed she'd been stabbed seven times. This allowed his barrister to blacken Bowman's name and put her grieving boyfriend on the stand and accuse him of killing her. No time was added on.* Not long after twenty-seven-year-old Karl Taylor denied murdering thirty-one-year-old businesswoman Kate Beagley by claiming he carried a knife to their date because he was feel-ing depressed, and that when it fell from his sleeve she picked it up and stabbed herself thirty-one times in the face, neck and throat. Why not? Didn't cost him anything. He didn't pay for his defence, and he didn't get time added on.

---

* He later appealed, claiming the trial was biased because jurors were told of his previous violent sexual assaults. The Court of Appeal said this was 'entirely without merit'. We still paid for it.

Why not a charge of aggravated perjury? Yes, it's subjective, but so are lots of points of law. Judge Jamie Tabor QC recently threw out a case against a man accused of violently robbing a woman because he deemed the victim, Denise Dawson, was 'too believable'. Suspects can lie as much as they like, but even if the court accepts the victim is telling the truth, they still don't get heard. It's insane.

Part of it is down to male paranoia. Whenever I asked a question about procedure the police parroted, 'Imagine it's your brother in the dock,' as if protecting the lone male was the primary concern of the judicial process. It goes right to the top. When former Home Secretary David Blunkett was in charge of amending the laws on consent, he ignored advice from the Law Commission recommending alcohol be included in the list of substances under which a man could not assume consent, saying he wanted to stop 'mischievous allegations'. This was a man forced to resign when caught abusing his power to help his lover's nanny get a work permit, who then began an acrimonious and nebulous paternity suit against his lover until DNA tests proved he was not the child in question's father. He was in charge of the Home Office. That's like making Bernie Madoff Chancellor of the Exchequer.

But the narrative of the poor man in the dock, subject to a woman's sexual caprice, is played out again and again. BBC and Channel 4 felt the need to do rape-trial re-enactments with a 'real-life jury', both with the same date-gone-wrong narrative as if this were representative of the central dilemma facing us, with the unsurprising outcome that when it was one woman's word against a man, you really can't be sure, so all defendants were acquitted. All the evidence from the police, however, says that rape, like all crime, is a repeat business. No man who's raped a woman and got away with it leaves the scene thinking, 'That was fun – I'll never do that again.' But it rarely occurs to women who've been raped that they might not be a one-off. Jill Craigie didn't discover until years after Koestler raped her that he was a serial offender.* The police told me they had numerous cases on their books of men who'd been accused of rape by three, four, five different women over the years, but each time, the CPS refused to prosecute, because taking the cases individually it was his word against hers.

Women would be far more willing to report rape if they knew that even if the man wasn't prosecuted there and then, they could proceed in a joint prosecution should further allegations come to light. But the CPS singularly fails to tell them this, and the legal eggheads can throw up as much hoo-ha as they like, but it's basic common sense. If a man found out his new best friend had been accused of rape, he might chat to him and agree it was a

---

* In an interview after publication, Ms Craigie said: 'Everyone kept going on about what a wonderful man Koestler was. One day, our friend Anthony Crosland said, "You know he's a rapist." Michael was shocked. I was relieved. I'd always thought there must have been others. But I still couldn't admit he'd raped me. Then, years later, I got rather drunk at a dinner party and it suddenly came out.'

rubbish charge. But if he heard he'd been accused twice
... three times ...? What if he discovered he also had a
penchant for violent porn and convictions for kerb-crawl-
ing, would he invite him to meet his girlfriend, or date
his sister? For some reason juries aren't trusted to make
these kinds of decisions.

Some male paranoia, however, is justified. The practice
of granting anonymity to victims of sexual assault but
denying it to the accused, thus ensuring that even if a
man is found not guilty his character will have already
been well and truly assassinated, is palpably discrimina-
tory. Trial by media does nothing but sell newspapers,
which is why not surprisingly this is not an issue the
media itself either raises or pushes.

Generalizations used when talking about rapists in the
media are counter-productive too. Every time a talking
head points out that not just common men rape, so do
men in suits, rather than allaying race and class prejudice,
the result is a wonky syllogism. Rape is committed by
men, men come from all different sections of society,
therefore every man could be a rapist – which, with its
echoes of seventies separatist feminism, frightens people
– and is of course nonsense. What it actually means is
the characteristics of rapists are not determined by race
or class, but by personality traits. Acquaintance rapists,
by far the largest proportion of rapists, have more in
common with the 'rogue traders' (or predatory traders
as they should be called) you see on TV – who are not
only selfish and greedy, and lack both empathy and a

conscience, but are also master deceivers – they smile nicely and accept cups of tea while stealing from the vulnerable.

There was a lot of interest a few years ago in the prevalence of what became known as 'the workplace psychopath' – the men and women who aren't violent and don't commit crime, but nevertheless behave psychopathically: they'll steal your ideas, stab you in the back, spread damaging gossip, whatever is to their advantage, and all without a pang of guilt.

But the idea persists that acquaintance rape is the result of changing sexual mores and gender miscommunication, and the truth, that a small number of men are committing a large number of rapes, and the majority of rapes happen when a woman is unlucky enough to find herself alone with the wrong man at the wrong time, is barely touched upon.

For TV, rape is there for lurid dramatic purposes and the body count of girls raped and murdered in shows like *CSI** is phenomenal. It's only in series like Paul Abbot's *Clocking Off*† that we get a realistic portrayal of acquaintance rape – such as in season three, where a woman's trust is established and then betrayed, by a man who everyone assumed was a great guy, and whose mother even knew ('Did it happen again?' she asks). But, despite

---

* The *Washington Post*'s Lisa de Moreas nicknamed these shows 'Die, Women, Die!'.

† Season 3, Episode 3, written by Matt Greenhalgh, transmission date 14 February 2002.

his best efforts, Paul Abbot can't write everything, and instead we get clichéd inaccurate rape stories churned out again and again.

Dispensing with this narrative cliché is in men's best interests too, as is the need to cut these rogue males from the herd. One approach to achieve this has been to change the balance of evidence. Bad-character legislation exists, but is at the judge's discretion rather than a mandatory requirement. (I asked the police how many women Strachan had attacked. They said that information was covered under the Human Rights Act. If they told me, and I told a third person, he could sue me for libel.)

The situation in the UK is so bad it's even received coverage in America (where thirteen per cent of rape reports end in a conviction). In the *Washington Post* (the *All the President's Men* paper), under the headline 'In Britain, Rape Cases Seldom Result in a Conviction', reporter Mary Jordan covered the case of a woman whose fifteen-year-old daughter had been raped.

'I gave police his name, address, mobile phone number, car registration – everything but his passport,' said the woman . . . 'I was basically begging them. He lived five minutes away from us.' It took three months . . . and a threat of legal action – before police questioned the suspect, a 28-year-old neighbour.*

---

* The police also lost mobile-phone records that contradicted the suspect's account.

Summing up, the judge told the jury to ignore the victim's young age and said the defendant was 'in a way a man of good character' because his previous convictions, for stolen goods and drugs, did not involve violence. The neighbour got off. So, in an English rape trial, a proven willingness to break the law, act selfishly and display no impulse-control is actually evidence of 'good character'? It's beyond absurd, it's Lewis Carroll.

The *Post* also reported with near incredulity the case of Judge Julian Hall,* who in June 2007 sentenced a twenty-four-year-old man to two years in prison for raping a ten-year-old girl, saying the girl had 'dressed provocatively'. (He's still in his job – and coming to a rape trial near you.) Of all the narratives/rape myths spun in court, 'she was dressed like a slag and asking for it' is by far the most powerful. In a 2000 study,[†] ten rape-trial barristers openly admitted their strategy was to portray the women as 'sluts'. Professor Temkin, the author of the study, said: 'They try to make out that the woman has acted foolishly . . . if she didn't consent she has brought this all on herself and she is to blame.'

And why wouldn't they – it works. Kerim Fuad

---

* If you saw the exceptional film *Chosen* about the sexual abuse that occurred at Caldicott School, in Buckinghamshire – this was the judge who threw the case out. He previously gave a paedophile a suspended sentence, ordering him to pay his six-year-old victim £250 compensation, saying, 'If it buys her a new bicycle, that's the sort of thing that might cheer her up.'

[†] 'Prosecuting and Defending Rape – Perspectives from the Bar', Professor Jennifer Temkin of Sussex University's school of legal studies, *Journal of Law and Society*, volume 25 issue 2.

(defender of more than a hundred men accused of rape), told the *Washington Post* he'd been surprised by some 'not guilty' verdicts – where jurors have been shown compelling evidence, such as blood at the scene or internal injury to the woman, and still not returned a guilty verdict.

For years men got away with murdering their wives, citing 'nagging', and killing gay men, citing 'homosexual panic' ('He made a pass at me and I lost control'), and now it's 'women are slags'. The woman of ill repute dominates the rape discourse. I've often wondered what would have happened in the first trial if I admitted that I *had* slept with a man I'd met in a pub. Where would Muttley have taken it? She was willing to disparage me for working hard, so what if actually admitted I'd had sex? Bridget Jones may have been all the rage on the page, but put her in an English court and she'd be demolished. In study after study, a quarter to a third of Britons say a rape victim is responsible for the attack if she was drunk or wearing 'sexy' clothes. (It's important to reiterate, she doesn't even have to do these things – all they have to do is portray her as such.)

If, as studies prove,* that watching even soft-core porn

---

* In 1982 Dolf Zillmann and Jennings Bryant of the Universities of Indiana and Evansville exposed 'male subjects' to explicit pornography – non-violent yet still depicting women in subordinate roles. Using statements such as, 'A woman doesn't mean no unless she slaps you', and, 'A man should find them, fool them, fuck them and forget them', they measured what they called 'sexual callousness'. Men in the massive-exposure group had significantly higher callousness scores than those who had seen no pornography. These tests have been repeated with similar results. 'Pornography and Sexual Callousness, and

increases sexual callousness, and with 40 per cent of the nine million men in the UK admitting using pornographic websites,* it's going to show up in statistics. As long as, unlike in America, we don't have the right to challenge juries, all you need is three of them on a jury of twelve and the accused goes free.

Let's not forget class. 'I think it's just common sense,' said one barrister, 'that if a woman looks like a scrubber she's going to get less sympathy from a jury than someone who looks respectable.' Who decides what a 'scrubber' looks like was not, sadly, clarified by this upper-class white person. But a working-class woman, a single mother, an unemployed woman, represented by a piss-poor CPS barrister is going to be hammered in court – and the rape barristers themselves pointed out the inexperience of lawyers hired by the Crown. 'When you have a junior person up against a well-paid and experienced QC it's just carnage.' One QC interviewed by the BBC said he no longer defended rape cases because it 'was too easy' to destroy women's credibility.

Why wouldn't juries believe these myths about women? The semiotics of pornography are everywhere, no matter what your age. Pencil cases with the Playboy Bunny logo sit next to Disney and Winnie the Pooh in W. H.

the Trivialization of Rape', Dolf Zillmann and Jennings Bryant, *Journal of Communication*, volume 32 issue 4.
* 2006 (IoS/Nielsen NetRatings).

Smith's* while *Girls of the Playboy Mansion* plays on cable TV at noon ('What she needs is an ass in her face,' gasps the woman in the trailer). Playboy have even produced duvet sets for girls ('single duvet with bunny logo in beautiful baby pink'). This from the magazine that gave us a cartoon where a large-breasted woman in a short skirt is looking frightened in the presence of two smiling men taking their trousers off. 'Well, I'm a consenting adult, and Charlie is a consenting adult – that makes two out of three!' reads the caption.

Forty years since sexual liberation, gay is now an insult and pimp a verb. There have always been double standards, but more than ever a girl is judged by her looks and ruthlessly subjected to the Goldilocks standard – she must be not too hot, not too not, but just the right amount. Those that are deemed to fall either side are labelled sluts, ho's, slags or bitches, or mutts and dogs. The proliferation of the language of derision for girls is depressing and relentless. Music videos heave with 'candy girls', porn-inspired wish-fulfilments who wriggle around making the men look powerful. Sexual bullying in schools – name calling, physical attacks, using phones to record attacks, sending porn, aggressive groping – is markedly on the increase. In the UK, girls under sixteen made up 31 per cent of reported rape victims in 2004/5; in London,

---

* Who have refused to remove it. 'We always take into account the level of knowledge, sophistication and maturity of the people we are marketing to, particularly children,' said their spokesperson.

almost half of all reported rapes come from under-eighteens. (We don't know more than that – the Home Office doesn't actually record all sexual offences against children. That's left to individual police forces, and despite the government being advised over ten years ago to collate this information, it has never been done.) ChildLine recently announced it had seen a huge increase in calls from children reporting sexual abuse.*

In the mainstream, porn's values and vocabulary have been digested to the point of ubiquity. In *How To Look Good Naked* (Channel 4) Gok Wan (giggle giggle) told a woman who was uncomfortable with her body (giggle giggle) she was going to learn pole-dancing! Radio 1's Chris Moyles called a female newsreader a 'slut' and female listeners 'dirty whores'. Although much covered, the significant thing about the Russell Brand and Jonathan Ross[†] debacle was how, at the time, the jokes about Brand fucking the granddaughter over a couch were deemed appropriate to broadcast, but those where Ross and Brand offered to go round to Sachs' house to 'wank him off' by way of apology were deemed not.[‡] Different rules

---

* A total of 13,237 children called the helpline in 2007/8 saying they were victims of sexual abuse – more than a 50 per cent increase over three years.
† Both self-declared fans of hard-core pornography and in Brand's case, prostitutes too.
‡ This is not about bad language. TV chefs and Billy Connolly are profane but they don't abuse. Even Gordon Ramsay never uses bitch, whore, slag, etc. Although as the comedian Russell Howard said, 'How can anybody get that angry about dinner?'

applied. Ross not only kept his job, he was defended at the 2008 Comedy Awards by Angus Deayton, himself caught with a prostitute in 2002. And these aren't even rap stars, they're wealthy white boys.

ITV also presents Katie Price as a role model ('she's a good mother') and gives us *Dr Who*'s Billie Piper as cool and sexy prostitute in *Diaries of Belle de Jour*. My cable company (Virgin) offers thirteen adult channels – and if you don't want to subscribe, there's free-to-view shows such as *Pornocopia, Porn Britain, Sexcetera, Inside Spearmint Rhino, Sexiest Naked Wild On* ('travel series going to the sexiest destinations on the planet'), *Celebrity Body Parts, Sin Cities* ('Ashley Hames goes on a global spending spree to see what's on offer from the world of prostitutes'), to name but a few. And where I live, the folk at the top of the hill are in danger of losing their sub-post office, while we at the bottom have just gained a brothel – five minutes' walk from a secondary school – on the main parade of shops opposite Londis, advertising 'Sexy Thai Girls – 24 Hours A Day!!'.

The most pernicious development in recent years has been the co-opting of feminist language by the sex trade as it seeks to rebrand itself as a legitimate 'industry'. Titty bars, prostitution and porn are presented as evidence of women's empowerment, not men's desire to make money. This co-opting has been going on for years, starting when Virginia Slims in the US drew parallels between smoking fags and strong women ('You've come a long way, baby'), and L'Oreal has used 'because you're worth it' to hawk hair dye for years. But the parade of young girls of late naive enough to think they're part of celebrity culture, wheeled out by the sex trade and trailed through Westminster to defend lap-dancing and porn, is breathtakingly cynical. When moves were announced to reclassify lap-dancing clubs as 'sex establishments' the industry jumped to. In a BBC news report on 4 November 2008 we saw that 'lap-dancers Lynsey Catt, Sian Wilshaw, Katherine Martinez, and Sharon Warneford presented a petition with nearly three thousand signatures to Number 10 Downing Street, on behalf of the association.' Wow! Nearly three thousand signatures, that's like, well nothing at all. But hey, they were all young and pretty so it made the TV news. (A recent petition asking the PM to force water companies to charge churches as charities rather than businesses had 39,788 signatures but, strangely, it didn't make the TV.)

Earlier in October, photographer Ben Westwood protested against the proposed ban on violent porn by parading two people (sorry, did I say people, I meant women), around Parliament Square dressed as 'slaves' – bound and gagged, in latex and chains. Again, it made the TV news – why wouldn't it? Free flesh on show.

But when is a sex industry not a sex industry? Well, according to Simon Warr (Chairman of the Lap Dancing Association), it's when it's a lap-dancing club. Giving evidence to the Parliamentary Committee for Culture, Media and Sports, he claimed: 'the purpose of a club is to provide entertainment . . . it's a place of leisure . . . the entertainment may be in the form of nude or semi-nude performers, but it's not sexually stimulating.' Luckily Peter Stringfellow was there to clarify things. 'Of course it's sexually stimulating,' he said. 'So is a disco. So is a little girl flashing away with her knickers showing.' It's a shame he didn't bring along a copy of his autobiography *King of Clubs*.* He could have turned to page 29, and mentioned the high jinks he got up to in the merchant navy as proof of his keen ability to discern sexiness.

> I wrote every day to Mum and Dad, and to a girl I pretended was my girlfriend . . . I put all my romantic fantasies in these letters, until her mother asked Uncle Sid to stop me writing them. Apparently they were too sexually explicit for a twelve-year-old-girl.

I know he's a ridiculous muppet, but it's no wonder the sex trade behaves so boldly when men like this are accorded the dignity of speaking to Parliament. Then again the Labour Party accepted a hundred thousand pounds from Richard Desmond, publisher of *Horny Housewives*, *Only 18*, *Big Ones*, and that noble contributor to race and equality *Asian Babes*, so maybe he felt at home.

When Andy phoned me in the new year, I could tell from the tone of his voice that it wasn't good news.

---

* Proof that I really will read the first thirty pages of anything.

'He went to appeal,' he said. 'It's been upheld.'

Some judges whose names I never knew sat in judgement I know not where, and decided in their infinite wisdom to reduce Strachan's sentence to nine years. I don't know why. Strictly speaking, Andy didn't even have to tell me because as mentioned, it wasn't me v. him, it was the Queen v. him, and apparently the Crown doesn't think I need to know.

Andy is exactly the kind of officer you would want to work on cases like this, and he didn't try to disguise his annoyance.* But like all good police officers he's constrained by a system that seems determined to ignore, frustrate or undermine his best efforts.

Prisoners only serve half of their tariff, and taking off the time spent on remand waiting for the trials Strachan forced (where you get to wear your own clothes, have your own money and are considerably freer than convicted prisoners), he'll do just under three years' proper prison, and chances are, by the time you read this, he'll be free, and living next door to someone.

So even when it all goes according to plan, a serial rapist can attack a woman, deny it, force two trials, lie under oath and still get time off. What would they have done if he'd shown remorse and pleaded guilty? Sent him home with a packed lunch? There have been times in the

---

* It was the police who broke with convention who released the details of the Stacey Westbury case mentioned in the dedication, so frustrated were they by the CPS.

last couple of years where if you'd offered me a deal whereby I could break into Strachan's flat at three in the morning, terrify him, bust his face, shove a pool cue up his arse, bankrupt him twice and only serve three years I'd have taken it.

When I decided to go to trial it was because I was appalled by the 5 per cent rape convictions in this country. Having got to the end of the process I'm no longer appalled – I'm amazed. Wow, that high? The government can tinker with the mechanisms of the courts as much as it likes (and as much as the judges will allow), but it won't make any difference if the police don't investigate sex crimes properly, the CPS doesn't prosecute them vigorously and the judges don't use legislation already in place to conduct trials. Even then it will be pointless as long as it's acceptable to routinely portray women both inside and outside court as self-serving sluts, whose primary value lies in their body parts.

The stories we tell each other matter. Words can describe but they can also destroy. Millions of Jews died because of the 'Blood Libel', *The Protocols of the Elders of Zion* and the word 'perfidious'. Black men are still trying to shake off the image of the libidinous savage, and killing Arabs became a lot easier when US generals talked of 'nests' of Iraqi's insurgents, clearly comparing them to vermin.

The economic revolution started by Milton Friedman and his 'Chicago Boys' that started life in Pinochet's Chile, and then spread to the rest of the world via Reagan,

Thatcher, Bush, Blair et al., championing deregulation, privatization and the free market as absolute goods (and government as a necessary evil) has finally ground to a halt. Their greed is (as Aristotle noted) infinite, but to contradict Gordon Gekko, it wasn't good. Government by targets and soft regulation was meant to give us a fairer society – a third way – where, liberated by the state and serviced by the unstoppable ingenuity of business, we could all be dynamic modern citizens living in a cafe society (because everyone should live near Upper Street). Unfortunately business quickly realized it could earn more building drink sheds in town centres and lap-dancing clubs next to supermarkets than cafes on the high street, and bugger the social cost.

With the bottom dropping out of the hedonism market, and the rest of us left to sweep up after the bread and circuses, watching the 'No Bank Left Behind' policy play out from the sidelines, there is perhaps space for a quiet revolution. We are more than consumers, we are friends, wives, brothers, sisters, neighbours, voters, football fans, ballroom dancers, workmates, an infinite variety of complex social relationships – and we want our civil society back.

As to whether words can describe, I've done my best. My story's not exceptional, it's ordinary, which is the point – it could happen to anybody. But rescued by the welfare state, repaired by the NHS and housed by my local authority, I have an enormous well of gratitude to all those who helped me, and a great loyalty to this country. If what had happened to me had happened in the States I'd be dead by now. Their welfare net couldn't catch a fat man on the bounce, let alone a traumatized woman with a host of emotional, psychological and financial needs.

The temptation to block out a horrible experience is obvious. But if you don't, it forever affords you a personal sense of comparison. The trial was unpleasant, but it wasn't *hell*. It was a bee sting to a broken leg compared to being attacked. It's like my family weren't and aren't evil. Very few people choose who they become and how they behave. People find it hard enough to do simple things like lose weight or stop smoking – where the plan is simple and the objectives and rewards clear. Change is hard. There's a reason most people vote the way their parents did (or don't vote as their parents didn't). We react the way we've been taught. But a point of comparison allows you to say, 'Great, I've got somewhere to live!' and 'Wow! Clean water!' and really mean it.

Looking out over the estate, people seem to be getting along, but it has been a long hard winter, and we shall have to see what spring brings. Personally I witness more than enough examples of kindness and decency to keep me going. On the block to my left I can see Tony and Bill, whose flats are side by side. Tony, in his sixties, is Afro-Caribbean, his Afro dusted with grey, and Bill, late fifties, white, with Andy Warhol hair and roll-up to hand. On summer's evenings they prop up the balcony, chatting away, never looking at one another, gazing across the car park and gardens. They live on the second floor and Tony's wife is confined to a wheelchair. Our flats have a step in the doorway, and nearly every day, Tony knocks on Bill's door, and without a word, Bill takes a side of the chair and they lift her outside. On days when the lifts don't work the two men carry her down three flights of stairs, with a gentleness and care born of kindness and practice. It doesn't occur to them that they're doing anything special, which is what makes it special.

As for me, I keep remembering what my surgeon said after the operation on my nose. I pointed out that a shard of cheekbone still jutted into the cavity of the right nostril.

'When I stick my finger up there I can feel it,' I squawked.

'Then I suggest you don't stick your finger up there,' he said and smiled.

And fair play to him, he had a point.

Now if you'll forgive me, I really do have work to do.

As I was writing this I got news that my father had died. I chose not to go to the funeral, but a number of friends (mostly lapsed Catholics) told me I should mark the occasion. 'He was your father after all,' they kept saying.

So on the day and time of the funeral I lit a candle. Correction, I turned off the TV (I was watching *Frasier*) and lit a candle and tried to think of three nice things to say.

'Thank you for getting the *New Yorker*,' I said – growing up in a house with such a fine magazine was a boon.

I had another.

'Thank you for reading P. G. Wodehouse.' Likewise, I don't know what I would have done without 'Plum'.

Then I hit a dry patch.

'Thank you for being mixed-race,' I finally said, 'because it means I tan easily.'

I admit it's not the finest epitaph in the world, but at least it was honest.

How to Deal With Trauma Victims –
Some Friendly Advice

1. Don't try to pretend you understand by introducing a bad experience of your own. Getting raped isn't like when your mother died or you lost your job (unless these involved random acts of violence). Also it shifts the attention from them to how *you* feel. Accept that unless you've suffered something dreadful, chances are you *won't* get it, and admitting, 'I don't know what you're going through,' is a better conversation starter than 'This reminds me of when I crashed the car.'

2. Take your cue from them. If they're having a 'day off' from being traumatized and are acting 'normal', don't bring their brokenness into the conversation. ('Are you sure you don't want to talk about it?') Even if you think they're in denial, it's not your issue to force.

3. Accept that this is not something you can fix. If that makes you feel powerless (which men in particular find difficult), accept that *that* is your part of the burden, and your endurance of it, actively willing to put yourself in an awkward place for someone else, is your gift. Remember, however hard you find it being around someone traumatized, being traumatized is much worse.

4. Listen. If, having taken your cue from them, they want to talk, *listen*. Don't try and manage their feelings if you become uncomfortable. If the feelings expressed are of

hopelessness and despair, don't try and cheer them up because you find these difficult. Better to say, 'This must be excruciating for you,' than, 'You'll get over this.'

5. Unless the person is already religious don't tell them, 'God loves you.' It doesn't matter if you think this will make them feel better. Just don't.

6. Don't gossip. Even the best-intentioned people can sometimes fall victim to the lure of drama. Telling people who need to know and discussing it from a place of concern is different from telling all and sundry. Weeks after the attack, a woman I barely knew spotted me in a restaurant and felt the need to share how awful she thought it all was. At the time I was with someone I had chosen not to tell, because I wanted to feel normal, if only for an evening.

7. Recognize your strengths. You may not have suffered trauma, or be wildly empathetic or emotionally literate. But you may be practical and pragmatic: for example, I'm very good at filling in forms, and these are good skills too . . . You can offer to do shopping, sort out the builders, phone the credit-card company – whatever needs attending to. Better still, don't offer, just do it.

8. Don't present a traumatized person with open-ended choices, e.g. don't say, 'I don't know, what would you like to do?' Decision-making is stressful if your emotions are all over the place. Appropriate suggestions, such as 'We could go to the park or rent a video,' or 'We can stay

in and I'll cook,' make life easier, and indicate care and effort.

9. Find someone to talk to. If you're going to spend time with a traumatized person, you're going to need to debrief. If you're a human being, you will get upset. It's normal and it's appropriate

10. Don't give up. Even if it gets boring. A lot of victims feel the pressure to 'get over' what's happened to them. Rape, like losing a child, is not something you get over in a set length of time. It's something you have to learn how to live with.

References

'The Afterlife of Arthur Koestler', Julian Barnes, *New York Review of Books*, volume 47, number 2: February 10, 2000, http://www.nybooks.com/articles/article-preview?article_id=221

'Morality and Arthur Koestler', David Cesarani, reply by Julian Barnes, *New York Review of Books*, volume 47, number 7: April 27, 2000, http://www.nybooks.com/articles/125

'Storm as Raphael defends rapist Koestler', David Lister, *Independent*, Tuesday, 23 February 1999, http://www.independent.co.uk/news/storm-as-raphael-defends-rapist-koestler-1072601.html

You Can Heal Your Life, Louise L. Hay (Eden Grove Editions, 1984)

Thank-yous

Without whom nothing would have been possible.

To the finest, funniest and most tolerant friends in the world – Barb, Russell, Christine, Garry, Marsha ('Where would we be without Marsha?') Chrispy and Judy, Reggie-Bear, Amanda, Helen, Suki, Martin and Kelly, Paul (N.C.D.) and Janine, and Peri.

In rescue patrol, thanks to Sara Nyandoro, Anne Thomas (the Welsh Wizard) and everyone at MIND, Claire at Just Talk, all the doctors and nurses at the NHS, and belatedly, the Atlee Government. Special thanks to the best neighbours a woman could have, Pat and Margaret, David Daley, Billy Boy, Derek the Painter and of course Louis the Man.

Thanks and enormous respect to DC Andy Lawrence and DC Donna Mitchell at the Metropolitan Police, for kindness and diligence above the call of duty, not forgetting Gerry and the miracle workers at the Fingerprint Bureau, New Scotland Yard.

Thanks also to Ursula Kenny and Roger Alton at the *Observer*. And last but not least, for their tireless help and support, agents Tally Garner and Gordon Wise at Curtis Brown, George Morley, my editor, for her first-rate guidance and forbearance and Dusty Miller for all her hard work.

Thank you, one and all.

Abi Grant 4 March 2009